Antony Lenti

Banker, Traitor, Scapegoat, Spy?

The Troublesome Case of Sir Edgar Speyer

An Episode of The Great War

With a Foreword by Sir Louis Blom-Cooper, QC

First published in Great Britain in 2013 by
Haus Publishing Ltd
70 Cadogan Place
London SW1X 9AH
www.hauspublishing.com

A CIP catalogue record for this book is available from the British Library

ISBN 978-1-908323-11-8

Typeset in Berkeley by MacGuru Ltd

Printed by CPI Group (UK) Ltd, Croydon, CR0 4YY

in memoriam
Roger Asbury (4/10/1920–11/03/2011)
happy warrior 1939–1945

A merry heart maketh a cheerful countenance

ANTONY LENTIN is a Senior Member of Wolfson College, Cambridge, a Fellow of the Royal Historical Society and a Barrister. Formerly a Professor of History and Law Tutor at the Open University, he is the author of *Guilt at Versailles: Lloyd George and the Pre-History of Appeasement* (1985), *Lloyd George and the Lost Peace* (2001), *The Last Political Law Lord: Lord Sumner (1859–1934)* (2009) and *General Smuts* (2010). He has published widely on 18th-century Russia and has edited *The Odes of Horace* for Wordsworth Classics.

Contents

List of Illustrations

Acknowledgements

Thanks and acknowledgements are due to Mr John Abbott; Mr Hugo Beit; Miss Naomi Boneham (Thomas H Manning Polar Archives, Scott Polar Research Institute, Cambridge); The Bodleian Library, Oxford and Mr Christopher Osborn (Margot Asquith Papers); The British Library (Lord Reading Papers); Mr David Cane; Mr Colin Harris (Bodleian Library, Oxford); to Mr George Liebmann for information on Edgar and James Speyer; Professor Margaret Macmillan for facilitating a stay at St Antony's College, Oxford, under a 'twinning' agreement with Wolfson College, Cambridge; Mrs Sarah Maspero (Hartley Library, University of Southampton); Professor James Moore; Mr David Murrell and Ms Susan Smith (Sea Marge Hotel, Overstrand); the National Archives, Kew (Home Office and Treasury Solicitor's Papers); Mrs Natalie O'Dell for information on the Orpen portrait of Edgar Speyer; Mr Arnold Rosen; Mr Peter Sigler; Ms Katalin Sinkovics (Killik & Co); Ms Jennifer Thorp (New College, Oxford); Mrs Gabrielle Thorp (for her brief but valuable comments on Leonora Speyer, her grandmother); Mr David Watson; Mr W S Robinson and Dr Theo Shulte. Finally I must record my gratitude to Dr Leanne Langley for indicating some useful sources of information and for setting me right on several matters of fact; to Ellie Shillito, of Haus, for her editorial solicitude; to Sir Louis Blom-Cooper for his generous foreword; above all to Dr Philip Webb of the Cities Centre, University of Toronto, for his patience, meticulous attention and informed and expert suggestions. For errors and misapprehensions responsibility is of course entirely mine.

Foreword

There is a danger, not to be underestimated, in resurrecting past miscarriages of justice, with the prospect that glaring faults of yesteryear will illuminate lessons to be learnt today. Very often the defects of such cases will have been cured by subsequent judicial rulings or legislative action. What remains is the intrinsic interest only; legal history has, of course, its own fascination. This book is a classic example of avoidable damage. Professor Lentin not merely revives an unfamiliar story of an incidence of social injustice, but also uncovers a lamentable tale, around the time of World War I, of political bigotry and social ostracism, born out of nationalistic hostility, partisan politicism and an undercurrent of anti-semitism – a lesson to us all. The chemistry of the legal process and political intrigue that engulfed Sir Edgar Speyer and his family needs unravelling. The ultimate procedure to deprive a prominent national figure of British citizenship and his position as a Privy Councillor, along with the citizenship of his family, makes for compulsive reading. Professor Lentin displays a helpful lucidity.

That Sir Edgar, with his German heritage and youthful background (he lived in Germany until the age of 25), committed indiscretions that warranted official censure cannot be gainsaid, although, significantly, there were never any criminal proceedings for offences relating to association with, and even indirect assistance to, an enemy with whom Britain had been at war. But did those matters, which were intrinsically quite serious – they were more than public indiscretions – constitute 'disloyalty or disaffection' towards the Crown? The three-man Committee of Inquiry (a High Court judge (Mr Justice Salter), a county court judge, and a prominent citizen), in a fourteen-page report made to the Home Secretary in December 1921, long after the war had ended was singularly uninformative, beyond largely rubber-stamping the Conservative-dominated Coalition Government's submissions that Sir Edgar should be deprived of British citizenship under the alien and citizenship legislation of 1914–18. Public opinion at the time was divided, and nothing since has pointed to a clear verdict. Professor Lentin, with conspicuous even-handedness, inclines slightly to favour a record of 'not proven'. His authorship is all too judicious and modest. The lesson for us is to beware a process that was gravely deficient and at that time under-regulated, in two respects, by judicial review.

The Committee's conclusion that Sir Edgar's conduct (or misconduct, if you will) fell foul of the statutory provision of 'disloyalty or disaffection' was a total failure to apply a legal mindset to an odd phraseology. That terminology in the British Nationality and Status of Aliens Act 1914 (as amended in 1918) survives in the same form to this day by virtue of the Nationality, Immigration and Asylum Act 2002, even though the language is more than a little outdated. A more modern formula appears in the European Convention on Nationality, to which

Britain is a signatory but has not ratified;* and, of course, the Human Rights Act 1998 would nowadays come into play as a controlling factor over the granting and deprivation of naturalisation. Deprivation is still considered to be available to the Government as a sanction that can be taken against those who act in a way that is seriously prejudicial to British interests, over and above the operation of the criminal law. Be that as it may, the deprivation of citizenship has always been regarded as a very serious step, to be taken only in the most flagrant cases of deception or disloyalty. It is a sanction that has been employed on only a few occasions. And recent case law has affirmed the principle that the word 'disaffected', as well as 'disloyal', requires an attitude of mind – be it noted – towards the Crown to which allegiance is owed: 'To be disaffected is to be estranged in affection towards an entity to which one owes allegiance or with which one at least has a relationship'.† Loss of affection is not enough. Nothing like that appears in the Salter Committee report of 1921. If the Committee had approached the language of Parliament seriously and considerately – the same as any body would today and as the Committee should have done under the 1914/1918 Act – a result favourable to Sir Edgar should have been arrived at. Judicial review today would have seen to that.

---

* By signing the Convention, Britain has an obligation to refrain from acts which would defeat the objects and purposes of the Convention; ratifying the treaty would demonstrate an intent to incorporate the Convention into the country's legal system.
† per Pill LJ in *Secretary of State for the Home Department, ex parte Hicks* [2006] EWCA Civ 400, para 32

What is worse is that the Home Secretary of the day, with whom the ultimate decision lay, seems totally to have ignored the legal issue, in which he had had some advice to the contrary from a government lawyer, and adopted a stance that would not today have survived judicial scrutiny. The Committee's report in its introductory paragraph recites Sir Edgar's 27 years of life in England in glowing, if understated, terms: 'He was a very prosperous and successful man; he was the head of a great business [merchant banking]; his wealth was large; he was the friend of distinguished persons [including the Liberal Prime Minister, Mr Asquith, who publicly in 1915 had declared his confidence in Sir Edgar]; he was a munificent patron of music [he rescued Sir Henry Wood's Promenade Concerts – the 'BBC Proms' – from inevitable collapse]; his charitable bequests were many; he took an active and useful part in hospital management. He was created a baronet in 1906 and sworn to the Privy Council in 1909'. All this conspicuous philanthropy and contribution to cultural and public life in Britain – which included financing the construction of much of the London Underground – was deemed irrelevant by the Committee. If rightly so, it should not have been irrelevant to the Home Secretary of the day, although if Sir Edgar's *intention* to disaffection was the statutory test, his contributions to British cultural life were, in my view, a relevant consideration for the tribunal, and certainly for the Home Secretary. No longer a British subject, Sir Edgar automatically ceased to be a Privy Councillor. For reasons to do with official understanding about the Royal Prerogative (very differently understood today), Sir Edgar was not stripped of his baronetcy and title, although he never used the title thereafter. The Home Secretary was not obliged in the law relating to public inquiries (then or now) to accept or act in accordance with the Committee's recommendation. In a House of Commons debate, the previous Home Secretary, Sir George Cave, pointed out that the final decision had to be made independently of the Committee. Sir George rightly stated: 'The act is the act of the Secretary of State, and not of the Committee'. Peremptorily, and in a decision that would today be judicially reviewable, the Home Secretary followed internal advice that he was bound to endorse the Committee's legally unreasoned verdict. He was wrong.

The fact that Sir Edgar was driven into exile to the United States in June 1915, never to return to live in England, dying in 1932 aged 69, hardly merited the loss of British citizenship, and even less so, his Privy Councillorship – a sinecure to a non-politician. It all betokened of an unyielding prejudice against a distinguished man, at the very least totally harmless to the interests of Britain in 1922. If one needed evidence of unbridled bias, and moreover an irrational decision by the Home Secretary, Mr Edward Shortt, it was his decision also to deprive Sir Edgar's wife (a distinguished violinist) and their three teenage daughters of British nationality. It is a mark of splendid (if remote) rebuke to the Government of that day and age that all three daughters (who were British by birth) subsequently returned to live in England, two to live here permanently, the third in the vanguard of the US forces in World War II. That they were granted leave to remain in England is small recompense indeed.

We should be grateful to Professor Lentin for rediscovering an episode of World War I. The case of Sir Edgar Speyer has been described as a 'minor tragedy of the War'. So it was, but it was more than that. It reflected no credit on a legal system that had always prided itself on protecting the individual against the might of the State. It not merely failed one prominent citizen; it blotted its own copy-book. Moderately expressed, Sir Edgar described the deprivation of his British nationality as 'an unrighteous action' by a civilised nation long after the World War had ended, governing with, at the very least, evident vengeance and absence of humanity. As was said by the Trojan lord, Pandarus, a public administrator's mantra should be: 'Be moderate, be moderate'.*

Sir Louis Blom-Cooper, QC

---

* Act IV, scene 4, line 1, *Troilus and Cressida*

Introduction

Micat exitiale superbis
'A fatal thunderbolt strikes down the proud'.
Motto beneath a painted mythological roundel
on the ceiling of the Speyers' music room

This ... charge that you were a spy and a traitor
John Roskill, KC. Counsel to Sir Edgar Speyer,
28 October 1921

My interest in Edgar and Leonora Speyer really began in the music room of their great house at 46 Grosvenor Street, Mayfair, where I was drawn by curiosity about the case. The house (now the headquarters of an investment advisory company) has seen superficial changes since they left it in 1915 on what turned out to be, though they did not know it at the time, a journey into exile. The spacious music room, then a celebrated centre of London's cultural life, running almost the length of the house and forming its focal point, is now a boardroom, divided by a long table. The portrait of Leonora by John Singer Sargent which then dominated the left-hand wall has been replaced by a mirror. The elaborate pipe-organ which faced it at the opposite end of the room was removed from its recess and the gap where the pipes stood has been crudely patched over.

From the windows, the view of what was an Italian garden is marred by ugly extensions jutting out from the buildings opposite. But the Louis XV-style interior remains, with its delicate carved wood panelling and its high, painted allegorical ceiling. It takes little imagination to picture candelabras reflected in the mirrors, guests in evening dress, and the music-making that took place there a century ago, for Leonora was a concert violinist and music was at the heart of Edgar's aesthetic life.

The Speyers customarily offered hospitality to distinguished foreign musicians and composers who happened to be in London. It was therefore natural that when in 1906 the elderly Edvard Grieg came to London on his way to receive an honorary degree from the University of Oxford, Edgar and Leonora should press him to spend a few days at Grosvenor Street. Edvard and his wife, the soprano Nina Grieg, arrived in the morning. After lunch, they found themselves 'quite alone with our host and hostess' and 'fortunate enough to get to know them better'.[1] The four retired to the music room, where Grieg sat at the piano and played several of his compositions. Then Edgar and Leonora persuaded Nina to sing. Which of Grieg's songs she performed one would give much to know, for, as the composer noted with surprise, it moved Edgar to tears. My interest was heightened by this man of business who revealed a romantic sensibility.

In the first decade of the 20th century the name of Edgar Speyer was frequently in the news. Financier and entrepreneur, 'King of the London Underground', public benefactor, patron of music and the arts, a friend of the

Prime Minister, Herbert Henry Asquith, and his redoubtable wife Margot, a regular guest in Downing Street, Edgar was a known figure in London society, respected and admired, a metropolitan Maecenas. Yet his name today is virtually unknown except as that of the first of two men, separated by an interval of 90 years, to be struck, at the Government's behest, from the roll of the Privy Council.*

Of German parentage and education, Speyer, who was granted British nationality at the age of 29, was not the first public man to become the target of national passions aroused by the Great War. Solely on account of his foreign birth, Prince Louis of Battenberg was forced to resign as first Sea Lord in October 1914, and the Lord Chancellor, Lord Haldane, was driven from office in May 1915 for his supposed pro-German sympathies. At the same time that Haldane quitted public life, Edgar and Leonora Speyer and their three young daughters left England to seek respite in America from a campaign of vilification that had pursued them since August 1914.

The peculiar distinction of the Speyer episode 1914–1922, and its historical significance, lies in the extraordinary pitch of malignity and the unrelenting persistence with which Edgar Speyer was singled out and demonised across a period of more than seven years. He became a

---

*The Labour MP, Mr Eliot Morley, was expelled from the Privy Council in 2011 after his conviction and imprisonment for offences relating to fraudulent claims for parliamentary expenses. Other disgraced MPs have voluntarily resigned from the Privy Council: Mr John Profumo (1963), Mr John Stonehouse (1976) and Mr Jonathan Aitken (1997).

marked man, in effect an outlaw; or rather the law was amended in order to make him one. The authorities left no stone unturned in their efforts to track him down. In 1921, after a four-year investigation into his wartime activities, a judicial committee of enquiry found him guilty of disloyalty and disaffection to the Crown and of communicating and trading with the enemy. He was stripped of his British citizenship and his membership of the Privy Council. He returned to America, this time for good. The proceedings against him, followed through at the highest levels, furnish a unique and disturbing example of the coordinated concentration of state power – responding to press, political and popular forces at a time of supreme national crisis – against an individual.

The good man brought low, the generous benefactor repaid with rank ingratitude – the theme is as old as Shakespeare's *Timon* or the Book of Job. The *Morning Post*, which had headed the pack of press organs to hound and harry him out of the country, showed more humanity on his death in 1932, when it described 'the downfall of Sir Edgar Speyer' as 'one of the minor trage-dies of the war'.[2] That, by any reckoning, and whatever view one may take of the case, is fair comment.

But how far was Edgar without fault in all this? The judicial verdict was unequivocal and pronounced with 'no doubt whatever'.[3] His conduct was reviled by the press as 'one of the most odious chapters of the war'.[4] *The Times* denounced him as a traitor, lucky to escape the hangman's noose, the *Irish Times* maintaining that 'throughout his eventful life Sir Edgar Speyer was consis-tently loyal to the Fatherland'.[5] But Speyer himself, far from bowing his head in shame, indignantly repudiated what he called the 'monstrous conclusions' of 'this partisan report', whose findings he dismissed as 'trivial beyond words'. In a strangely biblical expression, he blamed 'this unrighteous action'[6] on the Government that had set it in motion, whom he challenged to publish the evidence and let the public judge for itself.

Guilty or not guilty? Villain or victim? Scapegoat of nationalistic war-fever or one of Germany's most 'highly placed spies'[7] and a traitor to his adopted country? Opinion has wavered: tentative, ambivalent and uncertain. A brief but luminous cameo of the episode, some half dozen pages in all, appeared in 1932 in E F Benson's *As We Are*. In his sympathetic account, the author, who knew and liked the Speyers, nevertheless assumed that 'no doubt the sentence was just'.[8] By contrast Herbert Grimsditch, author of the 1949 entry on Speyer in the *Dictionary of National Biography*, suggested: 'It may be that he was guilty of no more than minor technical offences'. Presumably on that basis, Dr C C Aronsfeld somewhat optimistically asserted in 1956 that 'posterity seems to have sustained' Speyer's 'forceful demurrer'.[9] Professor Michael Brock, however, rejoined in 1982 that 'Speyer was not entirely innocent'.[10] More than 20 years later, in 2004, Professor Geoffrey Searle agreed that Speyer's conduct 'gave a rough justification'[11] to his detractors, and Professor Theodore Barker, revising Grimsditch's account for the *Oxford Dictionary of National Biography*, added, though without explanation, that 'there can be no doubt of his pro-German sympathies'. In 1997 *The Independent* newspaper described him as 'a convicted spy' and the BBC attributed his disgrace to 'collaborating with the Germans in the First World War'.[12] The weight of these verdicts hardly suggests a ringing endorsement of innocence. Then, in 2007, Speyer found a champion in Dr Leanne Langley, who described his treatment as 'a blemish on the nation, which deserves redress', and predicted that fresh research 'will surely lead to a posthumous clearing of Speyer's name one day'.[13] Sir Louis Blom-Cooper QC goes further. In his stimulating foreword to this book, he presents a trenchant and unsparing critique of the process that led to Speyer's condemnation by what, in Sir Louis's opinion, was a gross miscarriage of justice. Such comment from this distinguished lawyer suggests that the case would be a *cause célèbre* were it not so little known.

But where does all this leave Speyer and what is one to make of him? Perusal of these varying approaches left me, like Khayyám, having

> *heard great Argument*
> *About it and about: but evermore*
> *Came out by the same door as in I went.*

My own acquaintance with Edgar Speyer began when I was engaged on a biography of a great judge, Lord Sumner. I was drawn to Sumner's dissenting judgment in the case of *Rodriguez v Speyer Brothers*.[14] The wider background to that case intrigued me. I sought to find out more about Speyer, realised that my own passing account of him was inadequate, and a few years later

returned to him in a conference paper.[15] After this preliminary essay I followed up his half-forgotten story in
earnest.

What was called for was an impartial reconsideration of the facts. Whatever might be the outcome, the
challenge was one to appeal both to the lawyer and to
the historian. I saw my task as not so much to vindicate
Speyer as simply to ascertain, if that were possible, where
the truth might lie. 90 years after the publication of the
report of the judicial enquiry and 80 years after Speyer's
death, I had no axe to grind other than a desire to find
out what it was all about. But how to access the evidence
to the truth, one way or the other?

Release in 2003 of the Home Office and Treasury
Solicitor's Department files, including the transcript of
Speyer's trial, came to my aid and offered the opportu-
nity to attempt such a reconsideration: to raise the cur-
tain, so to speak, on events last examined 90 years after
the publication by a tribunal behind closed doors; to
retrace the events condemned, to ascertain what actually
happened and to place the episode in the wider context,
human and historical, of an eminent man swept from his
pinnacle by the cataract of total war.

As the subtitle suggests, this is a case-study, not a
biography. Too little evidence is extant for a rounded
character-sketch. Only scraps of correspondence remain.
In 2012 Captain Scott's farewell letter to Speyer was auc-
tioned for more than £160,000, but its public interest
derives from the writer rather than the recipient. In following the fortunes, or misfortunes, of Sir Edgar Speyer
during and after the Great War, the present account has

a focus narrower but more specific than that of a conventional 'life'. Traitor, scapegoat or spy? My aim is simple: to lay before the reader a candid record of events, and in the light of those to encourage him or her to decide for themselves which, if any, of these descriptions comes closest to the truth.

Cambridge
November 2012

CHAPTER I

La Belle Epoque

Vitae melioris ad usum

'To improve the quality of life'.
Motto beneath a painted, mythological roundel
on the ceiling of the Speyers' music room

A system of lines that would... render life more easy
and comfortable.

Sir Edgar Speyer on the completion
of the London Underground, 1906

A war... seems hardly conceivable.

Sir Edgar Speyer, 'Germany and England as Citizens
of the World', in *England and Germany by Leaders of
Public Opinion in both Empires*, (ed) Ludwig Stein, 1912

I n the opening chapters of *The Economic Consequences of the Peace* (1919), John Maynard Keynes looked back with nostalgia to a pre-war Antonine age of peace, progress and prosperity, when a man might invest his capital wherever he wished in a cosmopolitan, economically interdependent and financially harmonious world whose stability was grounded on the solid rock of the gold standard. The blessings of that world, and its apparently boundless prospects, were hailed at the time by one who thrived in it, in an article published in 1912, entitled 'Germany and England as Citizens of the World'. Its author was the Rt Hon Sir Edgar Speyer, Bart, PC. The article appeared in a collection whose title sufficiently explains his standing as a contributor: *England and Germany by Leaders of Public Opinion in Both Empires.*

Like the Rothschilds, the Speyers originated as one of the Jewish merchant-banking families of Frankfurt. By the late 18th century one Isaac Michael Speyer was the wealthiest representative of Frankfurt Jewry: indeed his riches outstripped those of the fledgling house of Rothschild. The founding firm of Lazard-Speyer-Ellissen was established in 1818. In the 19th century its activities fanned out across the globe, with branches in New York (1837) and London (1862). Under Gustav Speyer, the New York house, Speyer and Co, negotiated loans for the federal government during the Civil War and financed American railroads and enterprises in Mexico and Cuba. In accordance with Gustav's wish, its head at the turn of the century was his elder son, James, while the younger, Edgar, ran the London house, Speyer Bros. Their sister, Lucie, married Eduard Beit, who later took over the Frankfurt house now known as Speyer-Ellissen. James, Edgar and Eduard were all partners in each other's firms. In 1912, the year that Edgar published his article, Eduard was appointed Honorary British Consul-General at Frankfurt, a common arrangement in those halcyon days despite periodic Anglo-German tensions.

In 1886, having supervised the Frankfurt firm for three years after his father's death, Edgar Speyer, aged

24, settled permanently in London as chairman of Speyer Bros. He became a naturalised British subject in 1892. 'I was', he recalled, 'a very keen businessman'.[1] Under his management Speyer Bros prospered greatly, occupying a sumptuous Venetian-Gothic building in Lothbury, behind the Bank of England.

In 1902 Edgar took up a challenge which brought him into the public eye and also into some degree of controversy: to finance the transformation of London's transport system. London's rapid growth in the mid-19th century had attracted an increasing volume of commuters and visitors to the capital. The railways brought them to the periphery of central London, but the only form of transport from there to the heart of the capital was by horse-drawn carriage. The world's first underground railway, built by the Metropolitan Railway Co, opened in 1863. The tunnels were constructed by excavating a deep wide trench in the roadway, lining it with brick and covering it with a roof of brick or iron over which the roadway was relaid. The trains were hauled by steam locomotives. Despite complaints of smoke-filled tunnels, the Metropolitan and its rival the District line steadily expanded their tracks. The Circle line was completed in 1884, while extensions above ground reached such suburbs as Hounslow and Aylesbury by the 1890s.

During the 1880s, two important technologies combined to challenge the dominance of steam. The first was deep tunnelling through London's clay. Originally pioneered by Brunel, the technique was developed by Barlow (1869) and perfected by Greathead (1890), using a tube of cast-iron segments to line the tunnels and greatly speed construction. Deep underground tunnelling avoided the welter of sewers, gas-pipes and water-pipes. It also avoided the expense of compensating owners of some of the world's most expensive property for damage to foundations. In 1886 a new line was started from a shaft sunk below the Thames, with tunnels bored north and south, the prototype of the Northern line.

A second advance came in 1888 with the adoption of electric traction, first demonstrated by Siemens in Berlin (1878) and in use by the 1880s in Brighton and Blackpool. Electricity was the clean, modern and obvious alternative to steam: it was also thought that it would prove ultimately cheaper and more profitable, once the capital outlay had been met, though this would turn out to be an illusion. Two more deep-tunnel lines were opened, using electric locomotives to haul the carriages: the Waterloo & City in 1898 and the Central in 1900. By then, the idea of replacing locomotives with multiple-unit electric trains was rapidly gaining support: the Central line introduced them in 1903.

Numerous proposals were advanced for further deep electric lines, while the Metropolitan-District system came under pressure to electrify. The obstacle to immediate fast development was lack of finance. Parliament granted authorisation for the future Bakerloo, Northern and Piccadilly lines and some construction began, but funds to push them through were not forthcoming.

Around the turn of the century a remarkable American, Charles Yerkes,* arrived in London. Yerkes was a

---

* Rhymes with 'turkeys'.

dynamic American tycoon with a chequered financial background, who had nonetheless masterminded the Chicago elevated railway known as the 'Loop' and had tried unsuccessfully to establish a monopoly in public transport there. London offered greater possibilities and richer pickings. In 1901 he bought the District Railway and set about electrifying it, forcing the Metropolitan to follow suit. Yerkes had £1 million capital of his own and more from some American banking houses, but he needed far more to match his ambition of acquiring and electrifying an entire underground network for London.

Charles Yerkes met Edgar in March 1902 and put his ideas to him. Edgar responded quickly. In April, he formed an international consortium, the Underground Electric Railways Company of London, or 'UERL'. Speyer Bros and Speyer & Co were its main backers, Edgar Speyer and James Speyer were its chief directors and Yerkes was its chairman. The aim of the UERL was ambitious: to finance and oversee the electrification of the Metropolitan and District lines and the construction of major sections of what became, under the Company's ownership, the Piccadilly, Bakerloo and Northern lines.

Edgar's primary role, then, was to find the money to finance the UERL. Speyer Bros would market the shares on behalf of the Company, for which they provided a capital of £5 million. The UERL raised £15 million through a convoluted system – which even financial experts who examined it found abstruse – of shares and certificates, most of which were taken up by American and Continental investors. Further share issues raised a colossal total of £18 million by 1903. Commissions to the bankers, principally Edgar and James, were huge. In December 1905, however, Yerkes suddenly died and Edgar immediately took over as Chairman. As his responsibilities unexpectedly expanded, so his interest in the venture intensified. He saw the Company not only as a hoped-for source of profit which he must strive to keep solvent but also as a great public amenity, an agent of urban and social progress. The Underground became an end in itself.

Meanwhile, however, he faced a dire financial legacy left by Yerkes, whose ingenuity was exceeded only by his audacity. As a candid historian observes, 'if Yerkes had been an entirely honest, upright banker, much of the Underground system would probably never have been built'.[2] The exact nature of the relationship between Edgar Speyer and Yerkes does not emerge from the available evidence. It is clear that Edgar's imagination was fired by Yerkes' ambition and dynamism, but what was his attitude to Yerkes' business methods, which were by any standards unorthodox? How far he was privy to them and what part he played in them is not known. His own reputation was that of a man of resourcefulness and probity.

'Straphangers meant dividends',[3] Edgar had pithily predicted, but he was over-optimistic. The Company was vastly overextended and unable to meet its commitments, including heavy annual interest payments on the shares. Despite the huge £18 million capital investment, passenger numbers proved to be less than half those originally estimated – partly because of competition from bus companies. Revenue from fares fell far short of operating costs, which included the unanticipated high cost of fire-safety measures imposed by the Board of Trade. The situation had been compounded when Yerkes slashed fares in an effort to boost passenger numbers. Shareholders grew restive, awaiting the quick dividends promised on Yerkes's £100 so-called 'profit sharing notes' redeemable in 1908. £7 million of these bonds had been taken up, but the security on which they were issued consisted of shares in other UERL enterprises, some of doubtful value, and the value of the 'profit-sharing notes' had fallen by two-thirds.

In 1907, Lloyd George, President of the Board of Trade, was invited to open the Northern line, which now extended to Golders Green and Archway, despite the fears of Hampstead residents that tunnelling would damage the Heath.* At the celebratory banquet at Golders Green, Edgar tried to persuade Lloyd George to subsidise, municipalise or even nationalise the Underground. While 'other cities rendered active help', he observed, 'London stood alone in not assisting'.[4] Lloyd George was not to be drawn by the prospect of what he called 'socialistic legislation'. 'Sir Edgar Speyer', he replied, 'had tried to lure him into some of the loveliest traps ever set for a Minister'.[5] The London County Council likewise declined to take over the Company.

With American shareholders demanding their dividends and threatening bankruptcy proceedings as the date for redemption approached, Edgar bailed out the Company with £175,000 from Speyer Bros' reserves in order to pay interest due on the 'profit-sharing notes', and exchanged the notes for a mixture of fixed-interest

---

*The deepest of the Underground tunnels were 221 feet below Hampstead Heath.

bonds redeemable in 25 years and preference shares redeemable in 40 years. Settlement was reached with the shareholders at the last moment, Edgar himself addressing them. While 'it would be idle to pretend', he said, 'that the result of our six years' labours had not been very disappointing',[6] he pointed out that the biggest losers were Speyer Bros, as holder of many of the notes. He also kept the Company afloat by boldly purchasing in 1910 the flourishing London General Omnibus Company, whose profits could be diverted to offset losses on the Underground.

For all the unexpected difficulties encountered by the UERL and its narrow escape from collapse, Edgar remained resilient and optimistic. His energies and his imagination were bound up in Yerkes' inspiring vision – he hailed his late partner as 'the great master mind'[7] – of an integrated transport system for London and by his own involvement in its realisation. The UERL, which Edgar called his 'pet enterprise' and his 'child',[8] was the policy-making and managerial brain of the whole venture, and despite all obstacles, the 'Tube', which Yerkes had not lived to see, was up and running, a daily part of London life.

In the speed and scale of its construction and the comfort and modernity of its design, the Underground was one of the wonders of the age. John Price's electrically powered rotary excavators cut through the London clay at an average depth of 80 feet and at a rate of around 80 feet a week. Tracks ran both ways in separate tunnels lined with cast iron and concrete. They were lit by lamps situated every 40 feet. Power was provided by a massive generating station – Europe's largest – at Lot's Road, Chelsea, next to the Thames, along which a constant procession of barges delivered the huge amounts of coal needed to fire the eight steam-turbine generators. High-tension alternating current passed by cable to 24 sub-stations where it was converted to direct current at 500 volts and fed to the multi-unit trains through conductor-rails. Progress was spectacular. The Circle line was electrified by 1905 and most of the Metropolitan by 1908. The three new lines, Piccadilly, Bakerloo and Northern, were open by 1907 and amalgamated in 1910.

All three lines shared a common design. The rolling stock, mostly imported from France, Belgium, Hungary and the USA, was streamlined and elegant. The trains, consisting of from three to five cars, each seating 50 passengers, travelled at an average speed of 15 miles an hour, *including stops*, thanks to the increased acceleration provided by electric traction. They ran daily on average every three minutes from 5.30 am until 11.30 pm. Safety was ensured by American-style automatic signalling and braking, and the position of every train was visible to the signalman from an illuminated track diagram in his box. Access to the platforms was by electric lifts supplied by Otis, and every station had an iron spiral staircase for emergencies. The platforms were 300 feet long and 11 feet wide and were connected to adjacent stations by intercommunicating pedestrian tunnels. Forced ventilation ensured a constant flow of fresh air. The stations themselves, designed and decorated in the *Art Nouveau* style, had an exterior of glazed ruby tiles, featuring the well-known bar-and-circle logo.

These achievements were the fruit of Yerkes' know-how and drive. Except in finance, Edgar was no technical expert, but as Yerkes' successor at the UERL, he showed enthusiasm for every aspect of the gigantic undertaking, from raising the colossal capital to support it and devising and implementing the measures necessary to avert the company's threatened collapse, to approving details of the advertising posters, the map of the Underground, the uniforms to be worn by the transport staff and their personal welfare. He took pride in the Company's achievement, lyrically extolling the benefits of a network of lines that would

> bring the population of a vast area more easily and agreeably to their work ... render life more easy and comfortable and enable the poorer classes more easily and pleasantly to reach that happy land where houses ceased and where fields, trees and flowers began.[9]

In 1912 Edgar further consolidated the Company's control of London's transport by purchasing the two further Underground lines, the Central and the City and South London (now part of the Northern line). The *Daily Mirror*, styling him 'London's "King of the Underground"', pointed out that he 'finds himself, at the age of 50, the master-mind dealing with the mammoth problem of London's passenger-traffic'.[10] The same year saw the publication in the radical weekly, *The New Age*, of a not altogether friendly cartoon depicting a giant, mustachioed, self-satisfied Sir Edgar Speyer, legs astride, a train running between his polished black boots. Behind

Sir Edgar Speyer, 1912 caricature (J de J Rosciszewski, *The New Age*, 19 December 1912)

this image of a modern Colossus, however, the truth was that, because of the rapid spread of private motoring, unforeseen at the time, the Underground, whether under the UERL or any subsequent management, never became profitable.

Despite his involvement in the grandiose but loss-making Underground project, Edgar's own fortune remained unaffected. His prowess as banker and entrepreneur ensured that he remained an extremely rich man. There were other millionaires in Edwardian London, but Edgar was far more than that. In his opulent style of life, the extent of his munificence, the breadth of his cultural interests and his informed enthusiasm, personal engagement and generosity as a patron of the arts, he stood out as someone akin to a Renaissance prince, and his contribution to London's musical life knows no parallel. Of youthful, debonair appearance, slight and shortish at 5'5", with a 'very striking face' of olive complexion and 'brilliant brown eyes',[11] he was alert, active and decisive.

In 1895, Robert Newman, founder-manager of the Queen's Hall Orchestra, and its conductor, Henry Wood, launched the Promenade Concerts. Informal public concerts had been part of London life since the early 19th century, but little had been done to raise public taste until Newman and Wood made it their mission to make available the best of classical and modern music. One of the performers for whom Newton acted as agent was a young American violinist then in her twenties, Leonora von Stosch, a woman of remarkable beauty, character and talent. Leonora's father had left Germany for America as a young man, dropped his title, fought for the Union in the Civil War and married an American lady of English birth. He died before Leonora was born.

Despite her surname, Leonora was brought up as an American and was a celebrated 'Washington belle'. She had studied music at Brussels, Paris and Leipzig and performed with the Boston Symphony Orchestra. She made her London début on the first night of the 'Proms' in 1900 with a performance of Saint-Saëns's *Rondo Capriccioso* so impressive that she re-appeared at no fewer than six other Promenade Concerts that season. After an unhappy first marriage to an American, by whom she had one daughter, she lived for a time in Paris. Edgar and Leonora first met some time around 1900 in the Cotswold village of Broadway at a concert-party in which she was a soloist. Leonora obtained a divorce from her first husband and she and Edgar were married in Germany in 1902. Leonora was 30 years old, Edgar ten years older. Edgar had evidently joined the Church of England, for the ceremony took place in the English Church in Hamburg. Until she met Edgar, Leonora 'did not know a word of German'. Thereafter she was said to speak 'fluent but bad German' and in London she 'passed as an American'.[12]

A few months after Edgar and Leonora were married, Robert Newman went bankrupt. His ruin would have put an end to the Promenade Concerts had it not been for Edgar's prompt and spontaneous intervention. He stepped in –'to please my wife',[13] he said – by offering immediate financial and practical help. He set up the Queen's Hall Orchestra as a limited company, Edgar himself becoming Chairman, while retaining Newman as manager and investing upwards of £2,000 a year in the orchestra, some £26,000 in all by 1914. He thus saved the Proms by underwriting their losses and placing them on an assured financial footing.

Leonora Speyer *aet* 35, (John Singer Sargent, 1907). This portrait had pride of place in the music room of the Speyers' house in Grosvenor Street.

He did more than that. As the *Saturday Review* later put it, 'Speyer was out to make music, not money'.[14] He set out to make the best music available to the widest possible public, and he did so by offering almost absurdly favourable prices: the average price of a season ticket was fourpence a night. He set the orchestra on a new and professional foundation. Hitherto, members of the orchestra were only paid to perform on the night of the concert and even then they might engage a substitute! Edgar put a stop to this, and insisted on personal attendance at rehearsals. He encouraged and seconded Wood and Newman's ambition to improve the orchestra's quality and enlarge its repertoire. Wood recalled 'how delightful I found Speyer to work with. He was so sincere in his outlook, a lover of art willing to spend any amount of money to advance the cause of good music'.[15] A typical instance arose when Wood lamented the lack of a first-class oboe soloist. Edgar at once wrote off to the Paris Conservatoire. 'Come on!' he said to Wood. 'We will go over there next week and hear their best players. We will stay at the Ritz and enjoy ourselves'.[16]

In 1899 Edgar bought the leasehold on two adjacent houses on Grosvenor Street, Mayfair, and had them rebuilt as a single residence, No 46, by the fashionable architect, Detmar Blow. The exterior was elaborately faced in Portland stone. The principle rooms were variously designed in the styles of the gothic, the renaissance and the 18th century. The fittings including carved ceilings, some transported from Orvieto and the chateaux of the Loire. From a great hall, extended on each side by arcades, two massive staircases led to a music room decorated in the style of Louis XV, complete with a pipe-organ and a musicians' gallery. These splendours, matched by an Italian garden set with marble colonnades, produced in the heart of London a palatial dwelling fit for a princely banker, luxuriously fitted out and adorned with works of art, pictures, tapestries and statues.

In the music room, fixed within the panelling of one wall, the centre of attention was a magnificent full-length portrait of Leonora by John Singer Sargent, for which Edgar paid 1,500 guineas, the highest fee Sargent had yet received for such a commission. The background to the portrait was a 17th-century Flemish harpsichord exquisitely redecorated in the 18th century. It was in this room that Edgar and Leonora held their regular musical evenings. Leonora herself would perform on a Stradivarius or Guarneri, accompanied by a small private orchestra. At Overstrand, near Cromer, on the Norfolk coast, Edgar built a so-called 'cottage', in reality a large mock-Tudor country-house overlooking the sea and named 'Sea Marge'. Here too he hosted musical evenings

When, often at his suggestion, Wood and Newman sought to attract world-famous names to perform at the Queen's Hall, Edgar would pay the fees and offer hospitality at Grosvenor Street. He placed at his guests' disposal an entire suite of rooms, accessed by electric lift and overlooking the Italian garden. 'We live even more elegantly than kings and emperors', the elderly Edvard Grieg marvelled, when he and his wife were guests in 1906. 'We wade among masterpieces of art'.[17] A score of servants ministered to their wants. A limousine stood ready to whisk them around London. On the evening of his visitors' arrival Edgar would provide a special dinner in their honour, after which he would invite them to perform before a selected audience, which sometimes included royalty. Among those whom Leonora invited to meet the Griegs was the young Australian pianist and composer, Percy Grainger, whom she playfully called 'the village idiot'.[18] 200 guests were entertained at the dinner, after which Grieg took part in a recital of his own work which began at 11.00 pm. Grieg accompanied Leonora in a performance of his second Violin Sonata, Nina Grieg sang two sets of his songs and Percy Grainger played two of the Norwegian dances.

Edward Elgar had conducted the first performance of his 'Cockaigne' overture in the Queen's Hall in 1901. A year later, in a gracious, if slightly un-English letter, addressed to 'so eminent a musician as you are ... so deservedly popular and admired everywhere',[19] Edgar invited him to return for a repeat performance of that joyous evocation of Edwardian London. In January 1910, when Elgar was working on his Violin Concerto, he and his wife dined with Edgar and Leonora at Grosvenor Street. After dinner, Elgar and Leonora tried out the slow movement. It was so well received that they played it again. They rehearsed the first movement in May – Leonora predicting its 'worldwide success' – two days before it was premiered by Kreisler at the Queen's Hall. The following year Edgar financed the première of Elgar's Second Symphony. The appearance at the Queen's Hall in 1908 and 1909 of Claude Debussy was entirely due to Edgar, who sent Henry Wood to Paris to entice the reluctant Frenchman to London. 'Tell Debussy what you like', he told Wood, 'but make him come over'. George Enesco, also a guest in 1909, became 'a great friend' of Edgar. Everyone found the Speyers to be 'genial and charming'[20] hosts.

Richard Strauss had long been a friend of Edgar, and he and his wife, Pauline de Ahna, were frequent guests at Grosvenor Street. Pauline complained of a smoking chimney in her bedroom but the composer complimented Leonora at dinner on a 'well orchestrated'[21] dessert. At Edgar's invitation, Strauss conducted the first performance in England of *Ein Heldenleben* in 1902 to a packed and rapturous Queen's Hall. 'However many rehearsals I asked for in order to ensure a perfect performance',[22] Wood recalled, Edgar at once agreed. In the case of *Ein Heldenleben* there were 17 rehearsals. In 1905 Strauss dedicated his opera *Salomé* to 'my friend Sir Edgar Speyer'.

The music critic of the *Observer* hailed the Promenade Concert season of 1911, comparing modern audiences favourably with those of 40 years earlier, when the programme had featured little more than music hall items. 'This great growth in the popular appreciation of the finest music' was demonstrated by an educated audience that 'cheered itself hoarse'[23] at the Beethoven and Wagner evenings. By his material support and encouragement of Newman and Wood (he secured a knighthood for Wood in 1910), Edgar revived a cultural institution that extended and enriched the musical life of England.

Edgar told Wood that 'it had cost him many thousands of pounds to make Richard Strauss's *Symphonic Poems* known to England',[24] and the 1913 Proms season featured *Till Eulenspiegel*, *Don Quixote* and *Ein Heldenleben*, as well as Sibelius's *Finlandia* and such novelties as Debussy's *Iberia*, Ravel's *Valses Nobles et Sentimentales*, Vaughan Williams's incidental music to *The Wasps*, Frank Bridge's *The Sea*, Grainger's *Mock Morris* and even Stravinsky's *Firebird* suite. The *Observer* praised the season's 'remarkable success' and its 'educative influence'[25] on large and appreciative audiences.

Edgar patronised art and science as well as music. He financed the Whitechapel Art Gallery as a founder trustee. He coordinated the financing of both of Captain Scott's Antarctic expeditions, appealing for international donations. Without Edgar, neither expedition could have been mounted, for they were beset throughout by lack of funds. He personally donated £5,000 to the *Discovery* expedition of 1901–4. (The nearest contribution was a £1,000 gift from the Government of New Zealand). On Scott's return, he and Edgar became close friends. In 1909 Edgar agreed to serve as Honorary Treasurer of a fundraising committee for the *Terra Nova* expedition. When Scott set off on that second venture in July 1911, Edgar was among the small crowd of well-wishers at Waterloo Station. He had done his utmost to place the enterprise on a sound footing, but expenses continued to outrun the funds, as Scott acknowledged. Accepting that the expedition's assets hardly represented 'good security from a business point of view', he asked Edgar 'whether in the event of an overdraft you can get it guaranteed till I return'.[26] Edgar agreed to share part of the liabilities.

The news that Roald Amundsen was heading for the South Pole turned the *Terra Nova* expedition, essentially a scientific enterprise of great value, into a race for the Pole. Again Edgar lent his name to a fresh appeal for funds. One of Scott's last letters, written from his tent on his ill-fated return and found with him on his body, was addressed to Edgar. In this poignant testimony Scott acknowledged Edgar's generosity and set the expedition's financial failure against the tragic grandeur of its achievement:

16 March 1912

My dear Sir Edgar,

I hope this may reach you. I fear we must go and that it leaves the Expedition in a bad muddle. But we have been to the Pole and we shall die like gentlemen. I regret only for the women we leave behind.

I thank you a thousand times for your help and support and your generous kindness. If this diary is found it will show how we stuck by dying companions and fought the thing out well to the end. I think this will show that the Spirit of pluck and the power to endure has not passed out of our race ...

We nearly came through, and it's a pity to have missed it, but lately I have felt we have overshot our mark. No one is to blame and I hope no attempt will be made to suggest that we have lacked support.

Goodbye to you and your dear kind wife.

Yours ever sincerely,

R. Scott.[27]

Edgar lent his efforts to a memorial fund, part of which went to succour the explorers' dependants, part to commission monuments and part to found the future Scott Polar Research Institute in Cambridge.

Edgar's energies were not confined to the world of the rich, the famous and the cultured. His concern for the poor and sick went back to his early years in England, when he did voluntary work at Toynbee Hall in the East End. He was President of the Poplar Hospital, a member of the board of the King Edward VII Hospital, to which he donated £25,000, and chairman of the Nervous Diseases Research Fund. Nor did he treat these positions as sinecures. Once a week he attended the accident wards of the Poplar Hospital. He visited the bedside of every patient, and when that patient was the breadwinner, Edgar made a point of relieving the family's needs.

He was also President of the Royal Society of Musicians, a prestigious charity. He launched a fund to provide for retired members of the Queen's Hall Orchestra. Mathilde Verne, another friend in the musical world, wrote that to less fortunate musicians at the Queen's Hall 'his personal kindness was wonderful'.[28] He was liberal with favours and advice on investments. He lavished financial tips and bestowed the fruits of unsolicited vicarious speculations on friends and acquaintances.

Edgar's name appeared with almost monotonous regularity as a donor to every charitable appeal, from famine relief in Russia to the NSPCC. In 1904, on learning of the collapse of a penny savings bank at Needham Market in Suffolk, Edgar at once wrote out a cheque for the £5,700 necessary to restore their funds to the 180 modest depositors whose life savings had been wiped out. His action won him golden opinions. 'His deed is worthy of the Cheeryble brothers and we wish Dickens were alive to do justice to it',[29] declared the *Pall Mall Gazette*, while a servant in the Speyer household recalled of this episode that 'out of all the happy folks I think Sir Edgar and his family were the happiest of all'.[30]

The following year Edgar unexpectedly became the trustee of great largesse from the hands of another Dickensian figure, a Mr Bawden. Bawden was an elderly gentleman who had made his fortune in the City and had known Edgar's father. One day in 1905 he turned up at Speyer Bros in Lothbury, and when Edgar appeared, asked if he would do him a favour. In Edgar's words:

> I said 'Certainly Mr Bawden', and he pulled out a cheque from his pocket for £100,000, and he said to me: 'Here you are. I trust you to divide that money as you think best'. I was very much taken aback by this because it is one of the most wonderful things that ever happened to me in my life.[31]

While Edgar's public benefactions were legion, so too was his private generosity, which he made no boast of, being one of those who, it is no affectation to say,

Do good by stealth, and blush to find it fame.

The Speyers' generosity was spontaneous and unstinted. Their kindness to Henry Wood at a time of personal distress 'I cannot recall', he wrote, 'without a lump in my throat'.[32] Amid the splendours of Grosvenor Street, an atmosphere of kindliness, of bourgeois *Gemütlichkeit*, prevailed. In the intimacy of his home, Edgar was quiet, thoughtful and self-effacing, an affectionate and indulgent family man. Every year, for Leonora's birthday, he composed a miniature verse-drama in English and German, sometimes set to music by Henry Wood. He had translated into German several of Keats's Odes and a quantity of English verse and he wrote poems of his own, said to be of a melancholy and reflective nature.

Edgar played golf and kept a race-horse. He had occasionally hunted with the Whaddon. His name appeared regularly in the Court and society columns and he was enough of a public figure to become the subject of a Max Beerbohm cartoon in 1913. A zealous Sir Edgar casts covetous eyes on the scores of perambulators propelled along London streets by scurrying nannies anxious for their infant charges. The caption reads: 'Sir Edgar Speyer strenuously planning ways to a yet wider control of our traction'.

Edgar was a member of the Reform Club. He interested himself in Liberal politics and became an intimate of Campbell-Bannerman and especially of the Asquiths. As a member of a committee summoned to advise on reform of the Companies Act, he recommended a tightening of directors' liability for negligence. No doubt it was his contribution to party funds at the landslide election of 1906 that helped to win him his baronetcy that year at Campbell-Bannerman's instigation. In 1907 he was asked by Lloyd George, then President of the Board of Trade, to advise on the establishment of the Port of London authority. In 1909, on Asquith's recommendation, he was made a Privy Councillor. He publicly supported Lloyd George's controversial 'People's Budget' of that year and his name was high on the list of the 250 whom the King would have raised to the peerage at Asquith's request had the House of Lords failed to pass the Parliament Act.[33]

In the years before 1914, Edgar's Anglo-German affinities were more or less in equipoise and his loyalties undivided. He was a member of the German Athenaeum Club and as a patron of the German Hospital and German Orphanage in London, he was honoured by the Kaiser during his visit to England in 1911, with the Prussian Order of the Crown. In 1913 he was a leading contributor to the Kaiser's jubilee fund to celebrate the 25th anniversary of the Emperor's accession.

It may be that in that pre-war era Edgar and Leonora were living in a fool's paradise; but then so were most people. With hindsight, historians have descried seismic tremors beneath the crust of European civilisation. Few at the time imagined the immensity of the coming catastrophe. In the first decade of the 20th century, a time of intermittent Anglo-German tensions marked by violent oscillations of the diplomatic barometer from 'fair' to 'stormy' and back again, Edgar used his influence to inform Germans at the highest level of feeling in the British Cabinet, of which he learned at first hand. He sometimes acted as an unofficial go-between. In 1906, during the first Moroccan crisis, he warned the German ambassador in London, Count Metternich, of Britain's determination to support France. On a visit to Berlin early in 1911 he called on Chancellor Bethmann-Hollweg to emphasise British hopes for agreement on the Berlin-Baghdad railway and regretted that the Chancellor had never sought to make the personal acquaintance of the British Foreign Secretary, Sir Edward Grey. Bethmann-Hollweg, rightly assuming that Edgar would pass on his assurances to London, outlined points for settlement of the Berlin-Baghdad issue and said that he 'could desire nothing better' than a meeting with Sir Edward. On his return to London, Edgar warned Margot Asquith that Grey's aloof manner added to the impression held of him in Berlin of personal hostility, and said that if he would only break his insular habits and travel abroad more, 'he would not be so anti-German'.[34]

Norman Angel might argue in his celebrated thesis of 1910, *The Great Illusion*, that 'the delicate interdependence of international finance'[35] made war in Europe an impossibility; but the second Moroccan crisis, coming only six months after Edgar's Berlin visit, pushed that possibility to the forefront. In 1912, in his own published essay, Edgar too touched on what, like Angel, he trusted was the impossible, though clearly no longer the wholly unthinkable.

In this essay, Edgar hailed Germany and England as 'citizens of the world'. He quoted Goethe and Shakespeare with some complacency to illustrate the hoped-for prospect of ongoing good relations between the two kindred nations. All seemed reassuring in that golden age of continual progress save for an uneasy awareness, arising from the recurrent international crises, of the one nightmare prospect. That prospect loomed larger with Germany's insistence on challenging Britain's naval supremacy.

Enlarging, in words which echoed those of Angel, on the economic interdependence and mutual benefits of peaceful Anglo-German competition, Edgar held it 'inconceivable that the nations who are in the van of the progress of humanity and whose activity has brought such advancement to the world should recklessly destroy their great and civilising work by war'.[36] Edgar and a gathering of fellow Anglo-Germans were overheard discussing that appalling possibility. One of the company, in a phrase that epitomised their fear, observed: 'It will be a terrible thing if we English go to war with us Germans'.[37]

James Speyer was Edgar's elder brother by a year. He had settled in New York in 1885 to manage Speyer & Co. Like Edgar's, his operations were on a gigantic scale, floating large foreign loans, financing railway schemes as far afield as Bolivia and the Philippines. Like Edgar, he believed in 'international finance as a power for peace',[38] and he welcomed Churchill's proposal in 1913 of a 'naval holiday', a pause in the Anglo-German race to outstrip each other in launching bigger and better battleships. James's affiliations, however, were on the side of Germany. Only the year before, when a visiting squadron of the German High Seas fleet dropped anchor in New York, James threw a lavish welcoming party and had his naval guests conveyed by special train for further hospitality at 'Waldheim', his 100-acre country estate near Scarborough on the Hudson river.

James was hugely successful, rich, and munificent both in America and in Germany. He played a leading role in promoting cultural exchanges. He endowed the Theodore Roosevelt Chair of American history at the

University of Berlin in 1905, he founded the American Institute in Berlin in 1910 and established a Kaiser Wilhelm Chair at Columbia University in 1914. He was received by the Kaiser himself, who made much of him and wished to ennoble him. When James demurred at the honour, lamenting that he had no sons to inherit a title, the Kaiser exclaimed: 'There must always be a Speyer in Frankfurt!'[39] and in 1910 granted the title Baron Beit von Speyer to James's and Edgar's brother-in-law, Eduard Beit, who had two sons.

James's conspicuous ties with Germany proved awkward for Edgar in certain right-wing English circles where influential financier friends of Edward VII, of German and German-Jewish origin, notably Sir Ernest Cassel, were held in suspicion and disdain. It did not help that Edgar's English, though perfectly fluent, was heavily accented. 'The man can't speak English',[40] sniffed the Earl of Crawford, a former Conservative chief whip. The social snobbery common in Edwardian society was personified in Sir Almeric Fitzroy, Clerk to the Privy Council, who, deeply hostile to Edgar's appointment to that body, described him as 'a most characteristic little Jew'. When reluctantly swearing him in, Fitzroy made a point of thrusting the Old Testament at him, 'and thus saved the Gospels from outrage'.[41]

More ominous was a growing political animosity against wealthy German-born supporters of the Liberal Party, in a Tory party bitter after losing three successive elections since 1906 and passionately resentful of the 'People's Budget', the Parliament Act, Irish Home Rule, and Government policy, thought to be insufficiently robust, on national defence and national conscription. Passions ran high, political antipathies hardened into personal hatreds. The sinister tinge of a conspiratorial theory took root, propounded by such right-wing imperialists as Leo Maxse, editor of the monthly *National Review*. In their fevered imaginations, a 'Radical Plutocracy' of mainly German-Jewish financiers, members and beneficiaries of what Maxse called the 'Potsdam Party', was bankrolling the Government and receiving undeserved honours, all the time pulling the wool over the Government's eyes and carrying out Germany's business: promoting a pacifist policy while Germany prepared remorselessly for the coming day of reckoning. In these intimations of a powerful secret influence at work, a web of political manipulation behind the scenes linked to the operations of international high finance and with a whiff of the Marconi scandal,* there might be discerned a muted English echo of the Dreyfus affair.

In the legendary golden summer of 1914, however, the voices of such conspiratorial journalists were noises-off, irritating rather than dangerous. Relations with Germany were much improved. Agreement was finally reached on the Berlin-Baghdad Railway. Outwardly there was little to cloud the Speyers' happiness or to dim the lustre of their daily lives as glittering stars of the metropolis. In May, Edgar was taking the waters at Karlsbad. At the end of May, Leonora held a dance in the ballroom at

---

*The Marconi scandal arose in 1912 from allegations of corruption in the acquisition by members of Asquith's Cabinet through insider dealings of shares in the Marconi Wireless Company, the intended recipient of a lucrative Government contract.

Grosvenor Street with all her customary glitter and panache. She thought nothing of changing her dresses seven times in two days, Nina Grieg had noted in amazement, 'each one more splendid than the last'.[42] On 10 June, Edgar and Leonora were at a ball attended by a select company which included the German ambassador, Prince Lichnowski, and Count Mensdorff, the ambassador of Austria-Hungary.

Across three nights in mid-June, accompanied at each recital by the composer, Leonora was the soloist in the violin sonatas of Gabriel Fauré and Richard Strauss. On the 19th she played in Fauré's piano quartet. A week later, on the 26th, at a gala concert laid on by Edgar, Richard Strauss conducted the Queen's Hall Orchestra in *Don Juan*, *Death and Transfiguration* and *Till Eulenspiegel's Merry Pranks*. It was, said the *Musical Times*, 'the chief event of the concert season'.[43] Two days later, in a not so merry prank, a Bosnian student in Sarajevo levelled a pistol at the heir to the Austro-Hungarian throne and shot him dead.

Edgar's portrait by William Orpen was on show at the Royal Academy Summer Exhibition to critical acclaim. In July, Edgar took an exchange party of German schoolboys on a tour of London by Underground and bus. As one of four members of the Captain Scott memorial committee, he approved the design of a monument to the hero-explorer. On 15 July Leonora attended a musical 'at home' at Downing Street hosted by the Prime Minister and Mrs Asquith.

The season thus played itself out as usual in music, entertainment and public benefactions, and the Speyers betook themselves to 'Sea Marge' for the summer. A young guest, the composer Cyril Scott, dedicated to them a 'meditation' for piano entitled 'Sea Marge': a modernist piece, discordant and vaguely menacing. Meanwhile, something was afoot in the chanceries and war ministries of Berlin and Vienna. Whispering heads, grave but knowing, were bent over maps and railway timetables, ultimatums and military plans. Two short weeks, and out of the blue life would be utterly and irreversibly changed.

Churchill, then First Lord of the Admiralty, and his wife, Clementine, were old friends of the Speyers. Churchill's mother, Lady Randolph Churchill, had often been their guest at 'Sea Marge' and Winston and Clementine rented a cottage from them at Overstrand. They were holidaying there during those cloudless days in late July, when the coiled fuse ignited by the assassin's bullet at Sarajevo fizzled and crackled its serpentine way to and fro across the capitals of Europe until it exploded suddenly and uncontrollably in a world crisis.

Looking out to sea from the beach at Cromer under an azure sky, Churchill recalled: 'the North Sea shone and sparkled to a far horizon. What was there beyond that line where sea and sky melted into one another?'[44] Along the recently widened Kiel Canal the German battle-fleet made its way from the Baltic to the North Sea. The rapidly worsening crisis called Churchill back to London. At 'Sea Marge', Edgar and Leonora invited a worried Clementine to maintain contact with her husband by using 'the Speyers' splendid telephone' in Edgar's study. There, on 28 July, she waited anxiously to be connected at an agreed hour. Opposite her, above the mantelpiece, she noted a portrait of the Madonna, who 'gazes with melancholy eyes at the pile of business books on the writing table'. At midnight, Churchill wrote to her from the Admiralty: 'Everything tends towards catastrophe and collapse.'[45] Shortly before, he had sent orders to the Fleet at Portland to prepare to take up its war station. The following night, under cover of darkness, the 18-mile-long convoy of warships steamed northwards past the unknowing denizens of Overstrand on its long journey to Scapa Flow.

On Sunday, 2 August, Edward Marsh, Churchill's private secretary, a frequent guest at the Grosvenor Street *soirées*, paid a social visit to 'Sea Marge'. He found Edgar sitting out in the sun on the terrace overlooking the sea, listening to his three little pig-tailed daughters recite a poem under the supervision of their governess, Fräulein Klock. It was, he recalled, 'a perfect little picture of simple patriarchal German domesticity'. Two days later Britain was at war. Of Edgar, the children and Fräulein Klock, Marsh wrote: 'They were the last Germans I spoke to for many years'.[46]

CHAPTER II

The Blast of War

This war has altered everything. It is like a
tremendous hurricane, which uproots trees.

Edgar Speyer to his brother-in-law, Eduard Beit von Speyer,
12 August 1915.

This is no ordinary war, but a struggle between
nations for life or death. It raises passions between
races of the most terrible kind. It effaces the old
landmarks and frontiers of our civilisation.

Winston Churchill to Prince Louis of Battenberg, 29 October 1914

The outbreak of war gave immediate credibility to
the Cassandras, who might hitherto have been
dismissed as scaremongers. The war of which they had
assiduously warned for more than a decade had materi-
alized. Now they came into their own. Leo Maxse prepared for publication a collection of his articles from the
National Review, which he ironically entitled '*Germany
on the Brain*' or *The Obsession of 'A Crank'*. Scarcely had
hostilities begun when the Germanophobes gathered,
vulture-like, to swoop down on Edgar Speyer.

The attack began in the musical world. William

Boosey, managing director of Chappell & Co, which owned the head-lease on the Queen's Hall, had been a rival bidder for the Queen's Hall Orchestra in 1902. Since then he had stored up much rancour against Edgar, which now spewed out. After pressing Newman and Wood to cancel a Wagner evening at the Queen's Hall, he wrote a poisonous letter, published in *The Times* on 26 August, warning of 'the paramount position of many Germans in our world of finance', men with 'purchased titles', and control over railways and 'other means of locomotion'. The letter appeared under the extraordinary editorial headline: 'Highly Placed Spies'.

Boosey also served notice on Edgar terminating his tenancy of the Queen's Hall. It was, he wrote later, a 'necessary patriotic action'. As Edgar was a 'notorious German', whose musical programmes he described as 'aggressively German',[1] he could no longer be permitted to hold concerts there, to control the orchestra or influence its repertoire. German music should cease to be tolerated at the Queen's Hall. Edgar continued to finance the Promenade season of 1914 until his tenancy expired, and Newman emphatically denied that there was or would be any boycott of German music. 'The greatest examples of Music and Art', he declared, 'are world possessions and unassailable even by the prejudices and passions of the hour'.[2] But with the onset of war, the public mood, as Henry Wood recalled, 'was getting dangerous'. He felt 'intensely unhappy' for 'my friends the Speyers',[3] with whom he was in almost daily contact. Edgar sought to bring a libel action against Boosey after his grossly defamatory letter in *The Times*; but his solicitor advised that 'it was quite useless to attempt such a thing because in the excited state of public opinion no jury would convict'.[4] On the expiry of his lease, Chappell & Co took over the running of the concerts and the management of the orchestra, which they renamed 'The New Queen's Hall Orchestra'.

On the declaration of war, Edgar at once severed his partnership with Speyer-Ellison of Frankfurt, and a month later with the New York firm. This was in compliance with a legal requirement, reinforced by statute and amplified by royal proclamation, prohibiting trade, direct or indirect, with the enemy. At a stroke, much of the regular business of Speyer Bros was cut off, and this, as will be seen, came at a peculiarly difficult moment.

Furthermore, the activities of Speyer & Co in New York and in particular of his brother, James, placed Edgar in an exceedingly invidious position. First, Speyer & Co continued to do business with Germany, with all the main German banks and with Krupps and Thyssen. It had every right to do so, but this would lead in 1915 to its being placed on the Black List of firms with which Britons were forbidden to deal. Then James, without a thought for Edgar – the brothers, as it happened, were not on good terms – came out as an apologist, and more than an apologist, for Germany. In July 1914 he had been in Germany. The American intelligence services believed that he was 'interviewed by the Kaiser'[5] and that their discussion centred on America's attitude in the event of war. On returning to New York once war broke out, James told reporters that 'Germans regard the war as one of defence… The Kaiser did everything in his power to prevent it.'[6]

James had long been a friend of Count Bernstorff, German ambassador to the United States. Bernstorff was in Germany when war broke out. Returning to his post at the beginning of September, he was welcomed on his arrival in New York by James himself, who hosted a well-publicised lunch for him at the Ritz-Carlton hotel and entertained him overnight at 'Waldheim', where, it was supposed, discussion between host and guest aimed at furthering the ambassador's mission. In an article head-lined 'The Kaiser's American Agents', *The Times* described Bernstorff's reception as 'one of the first gatherings of the German clans' and surmised that James Speyer was 'taken deep into the councils of the German press scheme'.[7]

Bernstorff's arrival coincided with Germany's first setback of the war. The German dash for Paris was halted on the Marne. The Schlieffen Plan for the rapid defeat of France had miscarried. It was rumoured that Germany sought a way out through the intervention of President Wilson and that Bernstorff was the agent of this policy. One of James Speyer's neighbours and a fellow dinner-guest that evening at 'Waldheim' was a former US ambassador to Turkey, Oscar S Straus. Excited by Bernstorff's polite assent to his question, whether Germany would welcome American mediation, Straus immediately left 'Waldheim' to catch the midnight train to Washington, where he imparted this information to the President's Secretary of State. Straus had made too much of Bernstorff's affirmative reply, but the Allied press saw him as the dupe of a ploy concocted by Bernstorff and James Speyer.

From the moment of his arrival in the United States, Bernstorff lost no time in mounting a sustained propaganda campaign aimed at fostering American neutrality. He came equipped with large sums of money, which he deposited with Speyer & Co, to be used for propaganda purposes. Able, affable and assiduous in his efforts to woo American opinion, he issued regular bulletins and communiqués. The embassy at Washington was ever open to journalists, the Count always happy to be interviewed. Also in Bernstorff's team were Dr Dernburg, who set up an information bureau in New York, and the naval and military attachés, who were to recruit a network of spies and saboteurs in the United States, from whose activities the Count prudently averted his eyes.

James Speyer was thus far from what President Wilson exhorted Americans to be at this time: 'neutral in thought and deed'. *The Times* ranked him at number five, after Bernstorff, in what it called 'the General Staff of the German Press Campaign in the United States'.[8] The *National Review* described him as 'a rabid pro-German',[9] and the Earl of Crawford as 'one of our most violent enemies in the United States'.[10]

All this was bound to rub off on Edgar, who felt himself badly compromised by his brother's activities. 'You are to blame', he told James in a reproachful letter:

> When you arrived in New York, war with Germany had been declared, and I should have thought that as you are a partner in a German and an English house,

the obvious and considerate and wise thing to do would have been not to have allowed yourself to be interviewed and not to say, as the papers reported, that Germany was acting in self-defence, etc... That was soon known here and showed that you were taking sides.

James had capped this with his ostentatious hosting of Count Bernstorff. 'You evidently do not realise', Edgar continued, 'what harm this has done and is doing'. By this he meant 'the conviction which has now settled in people's minds that Speyers are acting in a pro-German way'.[11]

That was certainly the perception. Leo Maxse called attention to the 'unenviable notoriety'[12] attaching to Edgar from his brother. Michael Hicks Beach, son of a former Conservative Chancellor of the Exchequer, complained that Edgar's 'family sympathies (if not his own) are with the enemy'.[13] When Edgar resigned from Speyer & Co, *The Times* noted that he was expected to resume his partnership there after the war; while Max Aitken (the future Lord Beaverbrook and proprietor of the *Daily Express*) wrote to Maxse of his belief that Speyer & Co 'was undoubtedly financed from London in the early days of the war'. 'No doubt', he added, 'Sir Edgar Speyer has never taken his capital out of the firm although he has made a pretence of retiring. Undoubtedly his money is supporting Germany'.[14] This was untrue, but as Edgar was aware, people believed it.

Another of his relatives was also causing concern to Edgar. His 21-year-old nephew, Erwin, son of Eduard and Edgar's sister Lucie, was missing in France. His distraught parents sought help from James in locating him. At James's behest, Edgar consulted the American ambassador in London, who could do nothing. James urged Edgar to use his influence with the British Government. 'I have not stopped making enquiries', Edgar assured him. 'I am doing it all the time, and perhaps we will hear something by-and-by'.[15] As for approaching the Government, however, such a thing was not to be thought of. The British Expeditionary Force, already desperately hard-pressed, was suffering the most calamitous losses at Ypres. Margot Asquith, visiting the front soon after, wrote: 'The Ypres cemetery will haunt me till I die'.[16] Edgar continued:

> Certainly I have not worried the Government with the case of Erwin Beit. This would have been entirely useless and would only have irritated them. You don't seem to realise that thousands of people in this country are without news from those at the front, and every day we see long lists of missing – and these are English soldiers.[17]

Edgar had other worries. The war had a dire and immediate effect on Speyer Bros. Credit, other than credit realisable on the strength of the firm's good name, was not to be had. The firm held a million pounds of public subscriptions to the UERL. As part-author of the Companies Act 1908, which heightened the responsibilities of directors, Edgar was particularly sensitive to the criticism that might be levelled if such a large sum remained in the hands of himself and his partners, rather than in the safekeeping of a joint stock bank accountable to shareholders. He made repayment a point of honour and he at once put the process in motion. 'It was a task,' he said, 'which taxed my energies and resources to the utmost: but all the money was repaid during the war'.[18]

Before the war, Speyer Bros had backed certain overseas enterprises which had failed or were now failing. The Brazil Railway, which had seemed a most promising investment, 'turned out exceedingly badly' and went into receivership. It was 'the worst business that Speyers ever did', Edgar said. The losses were 'colossal'. British investors, especially in the City, lost 'a great deal of money' and were justifiably vexed, as Edgar was the first to acknowledge. 'My only consolation', he said, 'is that we lost more'. The St Louis and San Francisco Railway also went into receivership. So did the Missouri, Kansas and Texas Railway. Prospects for the Manila Railway were dismal. There were also the Mexican Railways, 'perfectly sound undertakings' in themselves, which had gone into default because of successive political revolutions. 'Never before in the history of the firm', said Edgar, 'had we three or four receiverships at the same time. Naturally the public felt aggrieved, and I did not blame them'. Never had Speyer Brothers 'had such a difficult time' as at the moment when war broke out, and in his efforts to repair the losses and satisfy investors – 'it took me weeks and weeks and many anxious nights'[19] – Edgar lost in a few months more than half his own fortune. Notwithstanding, in November 1914 he contributed £378,000 to the British War Loan.

While James Speyer was dining with Count Bern-storff in New York and at 'Waldheim', it did not escape notice that Edgar and Leonora continued to be welcome guests in Downing Street. Within a week of the outbreak of war, Rudyard Kipling, long a prophet of war with Germany, was asking the editor of the *Daily Express* to keep him informed of how often Cassel and Speyer lunched with the Prime Minister. Shortly afterwards he published his stern poetic warning – 'The Hun is at the Gate' – but he was no less alarmed by the Hun within the gate. The invitations to Downing Street continued to provoke the indignation of Leo Maxse and others. H.A. Gwynne, editor of the *Morning Post*, complained that Edgar was 'constantly lunching and dining there'.[20] Both the Prime Minister and his wife remained conspicuously loyal to German friends, and Margot Asquith became the target of press attacks on this account. One dinner-party in October 1914 at which the Speyers were present gave particular offence and became a notorious scandal. The Asquiths' guests included Winston and Clementine Churchill and the Marquis de Soveral, former Portuguese ambassador and veteran socialite.

Among the subjects of conversation at table was said to be the location and disposition of the British Fleet. When word of this got out, there was vehement indignation. Gwynne considered Edgar's 'relations both with the Prime Minister and with Churchill to be a disgrace'.[21] The Earl of Crawford, formerly Conservative chief whip, gave vent in his diary to his sense of outrage at 'this act of folly'. 'Speyer', he commented, 'is not trusted, his wife makes no secret of anti-British sentiments,' while 'Speyer himself', so Crawford claimed, 'has actually been watched, so suspicious are the authorities'.[22] Michael Hicks Beach believed that Edgar received 'confidential news'[23] from Asquith.

Crawford's informant was Soveral, a passionate Germanophobe, whose account may have been exaggerated and, conveyed to Crawford through a third party, may have gained spice in the telling. It is inconceivable that Churchill would have acquiesced in any genuine revelation of state secrets. The cause of resentment was perhaps not only what might have been divulged across the Prime Minister's table but also that in time of war Edgar and Leonora were at his table at all – and the supposed reasons for the favour they enjoyed. Pointing out that it was to Asquith 'that Sir Edgar Speyer owed that mysterious Privy Councillorship,' the *National Review* added mordantly: 'we have Mr Asquith's word for it that he has never given honours in return for cheques to the Party fund'.[24]

The Aliens Restriction Act and related measures under the Defence of the Realm Act, rushed through Parliament on the outbreak of war, required German subjects resident in England – now classed as 'enemy aliens' – to register with the police. They were liable to exclusion from 'prohibited areas', including most of the east coast, and in some cases to preventive detention in an internment camp. Britain's vulnerability to invasion and lack of provision for homeland defence had been part of the anti-German undercurrent since the turn of the century, much heightened by such fictional extravaganzas as William Le Queux' best-seller, *The Invasion of*

Lord Charles Beresford, c.1900
'There were several … who spoke against me: Lord Charles
Beresford for one'. Edgar Speyer

1910. Public suspicion now turned to outright hostility
against 'enemy aliens'. One such, on his way under
escort to a prison camp on the Isle of Man, recalled the
reactions of bystanders: 'They spat, they insulted, they
jeered, they threw things.'[25]

Admiral Lord Charles Beresford was a 68-year-old
former commander-in-chief of the Channel Fleet and
now Conservative MP for Portsmouth. Known as 'the
member for the Navy', a maverick and controversialist,
mistrusted in his own party but popular with the public
for his outspokenness, and uniting a daredevil audacity
with the mentality of an adolescent – Margot Asquith
numbered 'Charlie Beresford' among 'asses of every
kind'[26] – he was a practised intriguer with a sharp, fluent

and mischievous tongue. Long before 1914 he reputedly began each day with the greeting: 'Good morning! One day nearer the German war!'[27] Next to his own self-promotion, the battle-readiness of the British fleet was closest to his heart.

The public was expecting the Nelson touch at sea: a daring knock-out blow by the Royal Navy that would blow the Kaiser's fleet out of the water. Such expectations were shattered in September 1914 with the torpedoing in the North Sea of three British cruisers, *Aboukir*, *Cressy* and *Hogue* by a single U-boat, and the loss of 1,500 men. Beresford did not hesitate to attribute the sinkings to information supplied to the German Admiralty by spies in England. He did not respond when the Home Secretary asked for his evidence. Nor did he scruple to issue strident calls for the removal of his brother-officer and superior, the First Sea Lord, Prince Louis of Battenberg, as 'a German and a potential traitor, who ought rather to be interned'.[28] Churchill contemplated disciplinary action for such gross insubordination; but in the overheated atmosphere of public anxiety it was deemed inopportune to raise the temperature still further. Prince Louis, the King's second cousin and a naturalised British subject who had served in the Royal Navy since the age of 14, was duly forced from office. The spy-scare switched to other suspects. The Earl of Crawford railed at Edgar's unimpeded access to Downing Street. 'One's blood boils at these things', he wrote, 'while we know that communications are being made to the enemy'.[29]

Wireless telegraphy had become sensationally familiar to the public from its use in the arrest of Dr Crippen in 1910, from the Titanic disaster of 1912 and from the Marconi scandal, which broke in the same year. Lord Haldane, who had once described Germany as his 'spiritual home', became a prime suspect, one informant claiming that Haldane had a wireless set concealed behind a bedroom cupboard. Edgar, with a house at Overstrand on the Norfolk coast, fell straight into this class of suspect. It was rumoured that 'Sea Marge' was 'a stronghold of espionage'[30] and that Edgar, who was believed to have recently installed a wireless apparatus there, was in the habit of signalling to German submarines. He might equally have done so, of course, without the aid of wireless, since the house afforded an uninterrupted view of the sea, and he could have made contact in the fashion of spy stories, by passing a light to and fro in front of a window. From the start of the war, indeed, letters, both signed and anonymous, had alerted Scotland Yard's Special Branch to 'wireless installations', 'suspicious lights' and 'powerful motor cars with strong headlights' as well as to the presence, both at 'Sea Marge' and Grosvenor Street, of 'foreign employees'.[31]

At the end of September 1914, the Home Secretary Reginald McKenna received the following letter:

The Chief Constable's Office,
County Constabulary,
Norwich.
26th September, 1914

The Right Hon.
The Secretary of State,
Home Office.
Whitehall,
London, S.W.

Sir,

Owing to the many persistent rumours which have reached me in reference to the Right Hon. Sir Edgar Speyer, Bart, PC, of Grosvenor Street, Hanover Square, London, who has extensive premises at Overstrand, in this County, and in consequence of the suggestions made by the local War Office Secret Intelligence Officer, I thought it well to write to you on the matter.

So far, every possible attention has been paid by the Police to these premises and no suspicious circumstances have been observed, but it has been suggested to me that it would be as well to thoroughly search the premises, and that an expert should be detailed for the work.

In view of the fact that Sir Edgar Speyer is a Privy Councillor and a gentleman of affluence and standing, I judge it expedient to obtain your directions and observations before going further with the case.

I am, Sir,

Your obedient servant,

Egbert Napier (Major)

Chief Constable of Norfolk. [32]

The Home Office passed this enquiry to the recently established counter-intelligence department, later known as MI5. Its director, Captain Vernon Kell, replied that his organisation had 'gone into the case very thoroughly'. As far as Edgar was concerned, Kell had it 'on very high authority that he is quite all right'.[33] The Home Secretary confirmed that he too had 'good ground for knowing that Sir Edgar Speyer is loyal'.[34] It may be surmised that the 'very high authority' was the Prime Minister himself.

Not that Asquith's assurances would have done anything to satisfy Edgar's enemies or to allay their suspicions of what one civil servant, trusting that the Home Office would keep them 'under careful observation', called 'these paper British subjects'.[35] In any case self-appointed vigilantes were seeing to that. Edgar received anonymous telephone calls. Persons unknown scaled the roof at 'Sea Marge' and at Grosvenor Street, apparently looking for wireless installations. The servants heard them overhead. It was later put about that the tennis-court at 'Sea Marge' was intended as a landing-place for zeppelins!

At the start of the war, the fear was expressed that the London Underground might serve as a hiding-place for German spies and a secret depot for explosives. The Metropolitan Police conducted searches along disused tunnels, but their flashlights revealed no lurking alien conspirators; no latter-day Guy Fawkes in the person of Sir Edgar Speyer, twirling his mustachios in the manner of a Victorian stage-villain.

The *Financial Mail* sought to spread alarm over Edgar's alleged ability to sabotage London's transport system. Through his control of the Underground, it warned, he 'could throttle the whole of the communications of Inner London'.[36] His sinister tentacles might extend to the battlefield itself. Had not 500 of his London omnibuses been requisitioned to rush troops to the front? 'The German spy in our midst is causing a great deal of talk',[37] noted Margot Asquith, and the notion of Edgar as spy and saboteur was lent subconscious credibility by his surname. As Leo Maxse dryly informed readers of the *National Review*, Speyer Bros' telegraphic address was 'Spy, London', and Edgar's own telegraphic address was 'Edgar Spy, London'.[38]

Early in the morning of 3 November 1914, a squadron of German battle-cruisers under the command of Admiral von Hipper appeared off the Norfolk coast and fired a barrage of shells in the direction of Yarmouth. Little damage was done, the shells landing mostly on the beach, but the sensation was immense. This was the first naval attack on the English mainland since 1667, when the Dutch bombarded Sheerness and destroyed the King's fleet in the Medway. There was momentary panic even in Downing Street, and a fresh surge of spy-mania: wild accusations flared up across the country, heightened by the exposure of a score of genuine German agents. One of these, the notorious Karl Lody, had recently been publicly court-martialed and shot by firing squad in the Tower of London.

The proximity of Yarmouth to Overstrand – 30 miles – where the Speyers were then staying, the remoteness of the British Grand Fleet, then on its way from Northern Ireland and unable to anticipate or strike back at the enemy, and the rumour that Edgar had recently learned of the Fleet's whereabouts at the Prime Minister's own table – all this made his sojourn at 'Sea Marge' uncomfortable. He decided to return to London, 'not indeed because I thought I was suspected and possibly exposed to attacks', he wrote to his fellow Liberal, Lord Reading, now Lord Chief Justice, 'but because my wife has felt since the Yarmouth experience that she would not have a moment's peace leaving the children down here alone even for a day'.[39]

Before the war, Edgar and Leonora had been well thought of at Overstrand, where they had done many kindnesses to the locals. Now they were warned to keep away. Whether at Overstrand or in Grosvenor Street, however, they could not feel safe from a 'similar emergency', for 'such emergency may arise in London at any moment. I confess', Edgar admitted to Lord Reading, 'I am somewhat shocked and disillusioned at the lack of tolerance and confidence shown me in a country renowned for its kindness and true liberty'.[40]

Not everyone succumbed to spy-mania or rumours of military secrets dropped at the dining-table. The elderly and equable Lord Chamberlain, Lord Sandhurst, himself a frequent guest in Downing Street, was bemused. He supposed that there were spies, but not behind every tree and under every bed, as people seemed to imagine. 'As regards spies,' he wrote in his diary, 'I think the country has gone crazy about them', while 'as for gleanings of conversations being reported by spies, all I know is that I have dined with Cabinet Ministers scores of times and I've never heard any business conversation in my life'.[41]

But the next day he heard the Earl of Crawford in the House of Lords support calls by Lord Charles Beresford in the Commons for Germans to be removed from anywhere within 50 miles of the East Coast. *The Times* lambasted the authorities as 'criminally lax in their attitude towards potential spies upon our coasts'.[42] 'It is beyond question', Lord Northcliffe confided to the leader of the Conservative opposition, Bonar Law, 'that for some reason the Government are protecting spies – and spies in high places'. He hinted at donors of 'recent contributions to the Liberal exchequer'.[43]

The atmosphere of fear and suspicion revived in December with the return of von Hipper and the German fleet and the bombardment of towns on the Yorkshire Coast, this time with heavy loss of civilian life, followed in January 1915 by the first zeppelin raid over East Anglia. William Le Queux, ever attuned to the public mood, produced a timely book entitled *German Spies in England*, which appeared in February and went through six editions in 18 days. Cecil Chesterton, editor of the weekly *New Witness*, who had done much to inflame the Marconi scandal, now drew together the threads of a German-Jewish conspiracy which implicated Edgar. On a speaking tour of America, he did not deny, when challenged, having said in the *New Witness* that Edgar and others like him 'should be sent to a concentration camp and put to some useful occupation, like wood-chopping, so as to do for the first time in their lives an honest day's work'.[44]

From the day that war began, to their surprise and distress, Edgar and Leonora found themselves increasingly shunned by friends and acquaintances, cut by Edgar's City associates, liable at any moment to be subjected to stings and pinpricks, whispers and strange looks. 'It took the form', Edgar recalled, '– I do not know what to call it – of boycott'. It came as an unexpected blow to his self-esteem:

> It made my life perfectly miserable because I was accustomed to be trusted. I always had the confidence of my fellow men. I suddenly found myself in an atmosphere of absolute distrust and absolute suspicion.[45]

The London hospital boards on which he had served for many years wrote to inform him of complaints from other donors, warning that 'if I remained on the committee, subscriptions would be withdrawn'.[46]

He was heartened by private assurances of sympathy from colleagues, including the directors of the UERL, and friends not carried away by the current frenzy. Acknowledging a supportive letter from Sir Edward Elgar, Edgar expressed his appreciation of this 'friendly feeling and mark of confidence', as he wrote, 'at a time when [a] sense of fairness and proportion and logic seem to have forsaken a section of the people. I am happy to say', he concluded, 'that all our true friends have been both staunch and sympathetic'.[47] To Lord Reading too, who sent comforting advice at the time of the German bombardment of Yarmouth, Edgar wrote to express his 'sense of obligation to you for... the benefit of your wise counsel'.[48]

Not all their friends were true. They were snubbed by supposed old friends – 'pointedly and deliberately',[49] E F Benson recalled – and subjected, noted Henry Wood, to 'little slights and veiled insults'.[50] Instead of the customary welcome and respect, they now suffered or sensed the spiteful tongue, the barely suppressed sneer, the pointing of fingers, the monitory or mocking sibilants at their back. Even Edgar's portraitist, the sardonic Irishman William Orpen, dismissed him, perhaps ironically, as a 'bloody German'.[51] These fair-weather friends included guests who had only recently enjoyed the Speyers' hospitality at Overstrand that summer. They packed their trunks, they smiled their farewells with composure, and once back in town indulged in a spree of backbiting against their late hosts, from whom they could not distance themselves quickly or thoroughly enough. For Edgar and Leonora to appear in public now was to risk insult. In the *National Review* Leo Maxse objected that 'your millionaire alien walks abroad' with his '"Society" wife, who may be a common spy'.[52]

Leonora was generous and open-hearted as only Americans can be. She had opened up some of the outbuildings at 'Sea Marge' for the care of wounded French soldiers; but her offers to join organisations engaged in women's war work were chillingly rebuffed. Edgar was similarly mortified:

> I felt I could not do anything here. I would have been only too glad to have helped the Red Cross or any of those activities where my experience of business and my knowledge of languages might have been of use.[53]

As it was, he was able to accomplish at least two further good deeds. An old City friend sought his help in relieving the wants of an English student in Berlin, interned at the outbreak of war in the notorious prison-camp at Ruhleben. Edgar arranged through Teixeira de Mattos, the Dutch bankers with whom he had long done business, for moneys to be forwarded for the young man's benefit through the American ambassador at Berlin.

Then, in Edgar's words:

> A member of the Queen's Hall Orchestra, called Mr Winterbotham, came to me and told me that his little girl, aged thirteen, who was at school in a convent in Herk, Belgium, was unable to return to England owing to the occupation of Brussels by the Germans. He was most anxious about her, of course, and he wanted to get his daughter home. He came to me in great distress and asked my advice, whether I could by some means get hold of that little girl and get her away from the Germans.
>
> I thought the matter over and then said to him I would try to get the girl back for him, and I would try

Teixeira de Mattos, my Amsterdam house, and ask them to employ a courier, a Dutch subject. I thought it was possible by that means to get to Belgium to fetch Miss Winterbotham away from where she was and bring her to Amsterdam, put her on a steamer and ship her home. I am glad to say that I succeeded in doing that.[54]

So Edgar helped two young Britons caught behind enemy lines in the turmoil of war. He had also arranged for his children's governess, Fräulein Klock, to return to Germany for her own safety. The children, Pamela, Leonora and Vivien – not noticeably German names – aged 12, nine and seven, attended school for certain lessons. Then Edgar and Leonora were told that unless they took them out of school, other parents would remove their own children.

CHAPTER III

Hue and Cry

A total reverse of fortune, coming unawares upon a man who "stood in high degree", happy and apparently secure.

A C Bradley, *Shakespearean Tragedy*, 1904

Sir Edgar is what he says he is: a man who was driven into the wilderness

Sir John Simon, KC, Counsel to Sir Edgar Speyer,
4 November 1921

The war popularly supposed to be over by Christmas was going badly and had settled into the sanguinary stalemate of the trenches. Britons were experiencing a mounting succession of horrors, hitherto unimaginable, that brought home the reality of total war. The maltreatment of British prisoners-of-war in Germany, including civilian internees at Ruhleben, aroused deep anger and was debated in Parliament at the end of April 1915. German atrocities in Belgium were apparently authenticated by Lord Bryce's report, published on 12 May. The Bryce report contained much that was exaggerated, unverified or simply untrue, but its authority lent credence to the rumour, published three days later, that a Canadian soldier had been crucified.

Yet undoubted atrocities had taken place in Belgium, chiefly in the form of mass reprisals against civilians. Nor was there any denying Germany's wanton invasion of a small country whose neutrality she was pledged to guarantee, or her expressed intention to keep what she held. Underlying everything were Britain's appalling casualty-lists, the relentless, interminable, mechanised daily slaughter on the Western Front, horrifically exemplified at Ypres. At the end of 1914, the death-toll approached 90,000. By Easter 1915 it had risen to 140,000.

As the war intensified, so did feeling against the 58,000 Germans resident in Britain, who became enemy aliens on the declaration of war and were increasingly liable to suspicion as spies or saboteurs. 'Every German in London had an intolerable time',[1] Edgar recalled. The distinction between enemy aliens and the 6,500 naturalized Germans inevitably became blurred, and there was irritation at Ministers who insisted that there *was* a distinction. In January, Lord Crawford raised with Lord Chancellor Haldane the question of revoking the citizenship of naturalised Germans. He found Haldane 'very unsympathetic' and was irked at what he thought legalistic quibbling about 'complications of international law'.[2] In the *Morning Post* on 5 May, Lord Charles Beresford suggested that wealthy Germans should be interned as hostages.

A fresh spate of anti-Germanism erupted at the end of April with the deployment of poison gas by the Germans at the second battle of Ypres. It reached a crescendo with the sinking of the *Lusitania* on 7 May. The deliberate torpedoing, without warning, of a civilian liner and the death of more than a thousand passengers, including almost a hundred children, was, as Edgar said, 'a most horrible thing to do'.[3] Even if it was true, as the Germans alleged, that the *Lusitania* carried a cache of ammunition, this was unknown to the U-boat commander who targeted her in furtherance of the policy of unrestricted submarine warfare which was Germany's response to the blockade. The *Frankfurter Zeitung* hailed the sinking as 'an extraordinary success'.[4]

Popular outrage in England vented itself on German residents indiscriminately. Their shops were looted and ransacked. Top-hatted City brokers, heading a crowd of excited demonstrators, marched from the Stock Exchange to Westminster, to demand 'the immediate internment of all alien enemies, whether naturalised or not'.[5] Invading the Central Lobby of the Houses of Parliament, a precinct normally forbidden to strangers, they were harangued by Lord Charles Beresford, who declared that the most dangerous Germans were not the barbers, bakers and waiters, but those who frequented high society. 'I would put them all behind barbed wire',[6] he said. The Royal Exchange barred its doors to those of German or Austrian birth.

Rioting across London raged in all but two metropolitan districts. The right-wing press came close to condoning this explosion of popular violence in its demands on the Government 'to clear Germans and German influence out of England'.[7] The speed and depth of the decline from normal attitudes and values brought about by nine months of war, and the effect on English opinion of a policy of ruthlessness in which Germans seemed to take positive pride, was startlingly bought out by an editorial in the *Morning Post* on 11 May. Echoing the German 'Hymn of Hate' against England,* it declared:

> He who at this time does not hate Germany is incapable of hating evil and cruelty, and has no right to call himself either an Englishman or a Christian.

The worst of the London riots took place next day, 12 May, spilling into the West End and not sparing Grosvenor Street. Edgar received anonymous phone calls warning that No 46 would be attacked. He applied to the Home Office for police protection. A police guard was mounted outside his house, where crowds gathered to hiss and barrack such visitors as ventured to call. Friends offered to take in his children while the disorders lasted.

The next day, 13 May, saw a significant heightening in the anti-German temper. In the Commons, Bonar Law added his voice to the storm of condemnation of aliens. His attack on naturalised Germans could hardly have come closer to Edgar without actually naming him:

> There are Germans who became British subjects purely for business reasons, and who have not

---

*Written in 1914 by the poet Ernst Lissauer, for which he was decorated by the Kaiser changed in their feelings of sympathy for Germany. These men are a danger to this country [*cheers*], and in my opinion, the higher the position they occupy [*renewed cheers*], and the greater their wealth and influence [*prolonged cheers*], the more power they have to injure us. Therefore there is no class which should be more closely watched than this class [*cheers*].[8]

The same day, the *Morning Post* featured an editorial which named Edgar outright, emphasising his family and political connections. Asserting that 'the mob was in substance right', it reminded its readers that Edgar Speyer was 'a German by birth and education' and brother of James Speyer, who was not only one of Germany's 'chief tools in its anti-British campaign in the United States' but also a partner in a German firm headed by his German brother-in-law. It claimed that, like James, Eduard Beit von Speyer was close to Count Bernstorff, the German ambassador in Washington, and to Dernburg, 'the Black Hand diplomatist' and head of the German information office in New York, who justified the sinking of the *Lusitania*. Edgar had severed his partnership with the New York house, but the editorial revived an old canard in querying whether 'he withdrew his capital'.

The editorial turned to Edgar's friendship with Asquith and other Cabinet ministers. The Prime Minister and his colleagues, it claimed, should have broken with Edgar on the outbreak of war and should now 'rigorously cut themselves off from communication with people like Sir Edgar Speyer'. The same day, Margot Asquith noted in her diary: 'I get lots of violent and abusive letters saying I was pro-German. This is because I won't drop my German friends, Sir Edgar Speyer, Cassel, etc.'[9] The *Morning Post* declared that Edgar himself should have 'retired into seclusion' and 'given no cause for resentment or uneasiness'. It concluded:

> We should advise Sir Edgar Speyer and all in a similar position, for their own good, either to leave the country during the continuance of the war, or to live in such a way as to give no ground for the complaint that they exert any influence upon affairs, either personal, political or financial.

Against this fevered background there was founded a few weeks earlier the Anti-German Union, an organisation said to be 'inundated with applications for membership'.[10] Its founding-member and secretary was a Scottish baronet, Sir George Makgill, who had been at the head of the recent march on Westminster. The Union was pledged 'to fight against German influences in our social, financial, industrial and political life'. It called for legislation to preclude men of German birth from membership of the Privy Council and from holding any British honours or titles, and it demanded that 'British consuls shall be British subjects'.[11] This was unmistakably aimed both at Edgar Speyer and at Eduard Beit von Speyer.

The Anti-German Union was obsessed by the issue of the Privy Council. The Conservative MP Ian Colvin, a member of the Union, declared in the Commons that naturalised Germans should be expelled from the Privy Council. Among Makgill's first actions on behalf of the Union was to apply to the High Court for a declaration that Sir Edgar Speyer and Sir Ernest Cassel, both being of alien birth, had no right under the Act of Settlement 1701 to membership of the Privy Council.

The general situation had become so alarming for German residents in England that, for their own safety, Asquith announced on 13 May a policy of wholesale arrest and internment for all enemy aliens of military age. Germans long resident in England were rounded up at a rate of 1,000 a week and sent to the Isle of Man, where some thirty thousand were eventually incarcerated. Twenty thousand others, mostly the elderly and women and children, were forcibly taken from their homes and deported to Germany by way of Holland, ten thousand of them in the aftermath of the sinking of the *Lusitania*. They included Englishwomen married to Germans and classified as German by the Aliens Act of 1914 but with no other link to Germany and no desire to go there. Lord Robert Cecil, later well known as a leading advocate of the League of Nations, approved the Government's change of policy. 'The events of the last fortnight', he told the Commons, 'have made a very great change'. Hitherto he had been 'prepared to regard the ordinary presuppositions about men as being applicable to Germans'. But after the Bryce Report, the use of poison gas and the *Lusitania*, it was 'absurd to suppose that we have any right to think that the Germans are not capable of any crime'.[12]

The Prime Minister resisted calls, some from within his own Cabinet, for the internment of naturalised Germans. 'Nothing' he told his colleagues, 'would induce him to repudiate any grant of the full privileges of citizenship to all naturalised people'; and the Minister of War, Lord Kitchener himself, pointed out that not a single 'injurious action had been traced to any alien at large'.[13] Unless there was evidence to the contrary, Asquith told the Commons, naturalised Germans should be deemed to be loyal British subjects. Even the non-naturalised 'enemy aliens' he believed to be honest, decent people.

The measures decided on by the Government did not go far enough for the *National Review*, *Morning Post* or *The Times*, all of which complained that naturalised Germans were being let off too lightly, and should also be removed to places of confinement. 'And the rich naturalised alien, too, must go', declared Sir George Makgill. 'There is only one safe place for him – an internment camp.'[14] Even the *Manchester Guardian*, observing that naturalised Germans 'seem to have taken it for granted that their British sympathies were understood', advised them, 'in view of recent events',[15] to give public expression to those sympathies. The playwright, Sir Arthur Wing Pinero, called on prominent Anglo-Germans, if they were not to fall under suspicion, to show their allegiance by publishing so-called 'loyalty letters' in the press, and many hastened to do so.

On 13 May, a women's anti-German protest meeting took place at the Mansion House. As Margot Asquith noted with distaste, many militant suffragettes had turned readily from smashing windows and assaulting politicians before the war to handing out white feathers to young men not in uniform and to joining in the anti-German clamour. The meeting, chaired by the Lord Mayor of London, was addressed by the indefatigable Lord Charles Beresford. Beresford repeated his earlier unsubstantiated claim that 'there was no doubt whatever that spies were in our midst' who had tracked the *Lusitania* and sent word to Germany of her movements. 'But after all', he continued, 'the most dangerous enemies in our midst were the rich, independent, naturalised Germans in high social positions'. 'Such men', he claimed, were 'still Germans at heart' and they were 'not wanted here. They ought to have the good taste either to leave the country or to intern themselves somewhere'. He pinpointed 'certain German Privy Councillors'. What, he wanted to know, were such people doing in this country? If they were naturalised Englishmen, why did they not come forward and protest against German atrocities? Not that he would have believed them if they did, because, as he said, 'all Germans, whether naturalised or not, should be locked up', since 'naturalisation did not change the nature of a man'.[16]

The next day, Beresford attended yet another public meeting, this time at Chelsea Town Hall, chaired by Leo Maxse. Maxse denounced naturalised Germans, including Speyer, whom he did not scruple to name, as 'opulent, sinister, powerful, truculent Prussians'. Such men, he said, not only 'formed a sinister element in our midst', but might be 'a positive danger to the State on account of their intimate relations with leading politicians' and what he pointedly called their 'somewhat indiscreet families', who could prove a source of 'valuable information'. This clear allusion to Margot Asquith was confirmed when Maxse referred to Edgar's presence at the notorious Downing Street dinner. 'The right place for Germans', he concluded, to cheers, 'was Germany', adding grimly that 'if they did not care to go away, we should offer them the hospitality of barbed wire'.[17]

On 15 May, in his popular weekly *John Bull*, the scurrilous Horatio Bottomley came out with an infamous editorial calling for

> a vendetta against every German in Britain, whether 'naturalised' or not... You cannot naturalise an unnatural beast, a human abortion, a hellish freak. But you can exterminate it. And now the time has come.

Naturalised Germans, he said, should be 'compelled to wear a distinctive badge' and none of their children 'should be allowed to attend any school'. On 18 May, the *Globe*, a London evening newspaper, repeated Beresford's complaint that neither Edgar nor Sir Ernest Cassel had acknowledged 'their detestation of Germany's crimes'. Two days later a loyalty letter from Cassel duly appeared in *The Times*.

Edgar had just resigned from the UERL. An important Bill was about to go before Parliament. Its object was to amalgamate the Underground and the London tramway companies under the single controlling authority of the UERL. The Bill was controversial. His embarrassed fellow directors put it to Edgar that in the prevailing state of opinion it was likely to incur opposition unless he resigned. A number of MPs had expressed their intention to block it. Edgar could not deny the risk. He complied, but he was cut to the quick. He had always looked on the Underground Company as his 'child.'

> I started the Company. I was with the Company through all its great troubles. The Company had great troubles. That was just the time when we were hoping that the Company would emerge into success after 12 years of hard work, and then I was asked to give it up.

'This', he said feelingly, 'was the unkindest cut of all'.*[18]

Edgar did not write a loyalty letter, not, at least, of the kind which Pinero had in mind. On 17 May he wrote to the Prime Minister. He had resigned from the UERL. He had given up his membership of the hospital boards and his trusteeship of the Whitechapel Art Gallery. 'I have retired from most things after the attacks that have been made on me',[19] he reflected. Now he determined on a more drastic step. He tendered the resignation of his honours. His letter to Asquith, published in *The Times* on 18th, read as follows:

---

*'This was the most unkindest cut of all', *Julius Caesar*, III, 2, 181. Edgar knew his Shakespeare.

46, Grosvenor Street, W,
May 17

Dear Mr Asquith.

Nothing is harder to bear than a sense of injustice that finds no vent in expression.

For the last nine months I have kept silence and have treated with disdain the charges of disloyalty and suggestions of treachery made against me in the Press and elsewhere. But I can keep silence no longer, for these charges and suggestions have now been repeated by public men who have not scrupled to use their position to inflame the overstrained feelings of the people.

I am not a man who can be driven or drummed by threats or abuse into an attitude of justification. But I consider it due to my honour as a loyal British subject and my personal dignity as a man to retire from all my public positions.

I therefore write to ask you to accept my resignation as a Privy Councillor and to revoke my baronetcy.

I am sending this letter to the Press.

Yours sincerely,
Edgar Speyer

The letter caused a sensation. The veteran Liberal statesman Lord Morley, who had quitted the Cabinet in protest at England's entry in the war, confided to Margot Asquith: 'I admire Speyer's letter, snapping his fingers at us all',[20] but his was a lone voice. The letter was ill received by the press, though the press had complained loudest about German Privy Councillors, so that, as the *Financial Mail* noted, in offering to resign, Edgar was 'simply bowing to public wishes'.[21] The press in general turned Edgar's letter against him and mocked it as 'childish'.[22] *The Times* derided his 'ludicrous mistake'[23] in not knowing that only the King could revoke his honours. 'Sir Edgar Speyer', wrote one commentator, 'has not enhanced his reputation by his hysterical letter to Mr Asquith'.[24]

Asquith himself treated Edgar's letter with the utmost seriousness. Four days later he replied in terms of unequivocal support:

> 10, Downing Street, Whitehall,
> May 22
>
> Dear Sir Edgar,
> I can quite understand the sense of injustice and indignation which prompted your letter to me. I have known you long, and well enough to estimate at their true value these baseless and malignant imputations upon your loyalty to the British Crown.
> The King is not prepared to take any step such as you suggest in regard to the marks of distinction which you have received in recognition of public services and philanthropic munificence.
>
> Yours sincerely
> H H Asquith

This letter too was published in *The Times*, on 25 May, so that, as Speyer wrote shortly afterwards in reply to a message of support from Bernard Shaw, '"honour is satisfied", as they say'.[25] In the face of popular clamour, Asquith had taken a bold, principled stand. Four days earlier, in the same fighting spirit, he had challenged his colleagues to say whether they had ever known him to be 'influenced one way or the other by any paper or person. Did he care one d—n for the Press then or had he *ever* cared?'[26] Seldom, it might be felt, was the Prime Minister's cold contempt for press demagogy more admirably exhibited than in his letter to Edgar. This, his supporters might feel, was Asquith at his best and biggest, 'the last of the Romans'.

Asquith's defence of Speyer was the more remarkable in that it appeared amidst one of the gravest political crises of his premiership. The war continued to go badly. The Government, and the Prime Minister in particular, were blamed for what critics perceived as a lack of pace, vigour, foresight and grip. Asquith himself gave the appearance of slackness and complacency. There were insistent calls for greater effort, sterner measures, the more energetic deployment of national resources and the introduction of conscription. Bonar Law warned Asquith that unless the Government was radically reconstructed, he could no longer restrain his Conservative backbenchers from an out-and-out attempt to bring it down. That same day, the day that Edgar wrote to Asquith, Asquith himself had written to his Cabinet colleagues requiring their resignation, and was ensconced with Bonar Law in the formation of a coalition that would put an end to the

Liberal administration which had held office since 1906. 'Our *wonderful* Cabinet *gone*!! *Smashed*!'[27] Margot Asquith wrote to Haldane, chief victim of this sudden political revolution.

By including Haldane himself in his clean sweep, Asquith bowed to the demands of his Coalition partners for the Lord Chancellor's dismissal as the price of their cooperation and of his own survival as Prime Minister. No one had done more than Haldane as Minister of War to ensure the military readiness of the British Expeditionary Force. The nation owed him an immeasurable debt of gratitude: yet Haldane had long been the butt of popular clamour, amplified in the press, for his respect for German culture and the much-quoted remark that Germany was his 'spiritual home'. Bonar Law himself, as it happened, was also an admirer of German culture, but the press made nothing of that, and Asquith summarily sacrificed his Lord Chancellor in order to assuage Bonar Law's supporters and to ensure his own retention of power at the head of a Coalition in which, at his contrivance, the chief offices still remained in Liberal hands.

Haldane was, as Asquith admitted, 'the oldest personal and political friend that I have in the world'.[28] Yet while requiring his immediate resignation without a word of public apology or any acknowledgment of the unjust prejudice against him, the Prime Minister went out of his way to publish a forceful and defiant vindication of Edgar Speyer, whom Bonar Law had publicly denounced only four days earlier. This strange contrast in Asquith's conduct calls for consideration and will be returned to later.

One of the few to preserve a sense of proportion and decency amid the turbulent waves of wartime passion was the King. On the forced resignation of his cousin, Prince Louis of Battenberg, he had at once shown what he thought by appointing Prince Louis to the Privy Council. With the ousting of Haldane, the King once more demonstrated his own sense of values by awarding him the Order of Merit. Against this record of steadfast principle, we may be sure that in Edgar's case, Monarch and Prime Minister were at one in rejecting his offer to resign his honours.

The King was less successful in resisting the removal from St George's Chapel, Windsor, of the banners of German and Austrian Knights of the Garter, including his cousin, the Kaiser, the Emperor of Austria and half a dozen other crowned heads and princes, all of whom were now expelled from the Order. This he did on Asquith's advice and under pressure of agitation in *John Bull* and the *Daily Mail*, and for fear that 'the people would have stormed the Chapel'.[29] The King himself, a Coburger and Hanoverian by descent, his wife the daughter of a Duke of Teck, was not invulnerable to criticism.

Meanwhile the pressure on Edgar continued. H A Gwynne, describing Edgar's relations with the Prime Minister as 'a disgrace', expressed his intention 'to peg away at it'[30] in the *Morning Post*. Among the arguments he urged on the Government in an editorial headed 'The Case of Sir Edgar Speyer',[31] it was suggested that in German law Edgar might still be a German subject. Then Sir George Makgill's action against Speyer and Cassel was listed for preliminary hearing in the Royal Courts of Justice.

By this time Edgar was in the United States. On 26 May, accompanied by Leonora and the children, he set sail on the American liner *SS Philadelphia*, arriving in New York on 3 June. They escaped by a few days the appearance of the first zeppelins over London. But the malice of his detractors pursued him across the Atlantic. 'Sir Edgar Speyer has journeyed to New York', the *Financial Mail* proclaimed, 'for which London is truly thankful'.[32] From Australia came a withering attack on him as a German agent who had worked insidiously within the Liberal Party against those who warned of Germany's intentions. He had been 'a friend and flatterer of the fatuous Lord Haldane'.[33] Leo Maxse denounced him as 'Herr Speyer' and trumpeted the 'widespread conviction that German Plutocrats have been substantial contributors to Party funds – which would explain their immunity'.[34] It would have made no difference to Maxse and his like that a month after reaching America, Edgar donated a further £27,000 to the British War Loan.

CHAPTER IV

On the Trail

> Where did his sympathies lie? Let us judge him by
> his actions. He throws his Privy Councillorship in
> the Sovereign's face, and his Baronetcy as well; and
> are we not justified in saying that his sympathies, by
> that very action, showed themselves to be German
> and not British?
>
> Lord Wittenham (formerly Registrar to the Privy Council),
> House of Lords, 26 July 1918

On 23 June 1915, three weeks after Edgar's arrival in America, Sir George Makgill of the Anti-German Union made a successful preliminary application to the High Court in London. The Court directed that an order be served on Sir Ernest Cassel and Sir Edgar Speyer, under the ancient name of *quo warranto*, to show by what authority they claimed to be members of the Privy Council. While insisting that his client 'bore no animus against anyone in particular', Makgill's Counsel observed archly that Edgar had left the jurisdiction 'for his health or something else'.[1]

Six months later, in December, the full case came before the King's Bench Division of the High Court, presided over by the Lord Chief Justice, Lord Reading.

Makgill's argument was simple: Cassel and Speyer were ineligible to sit on the Privy Council by virtue of Section 3 of the Act of Settlement, 1701. The section was unequivocal:

> No person born out of the kingdoms of England, Scotland, or Ireland or the Dominions thereunto belonging (although he be naturalised... except such as are born of English parents) shall be capable to be of the Privy Council.

The case* was argued by some of the leading advocates at the English bar. Cassel retained the services of Sir Robert Finlay (soon to be Lord Chancellor). Edgar was represented in his absence by John Henry Roskill. The Court had directed that notice of the hearing be served on the Home Secretary as an interested party, but in complying with this direction, Makgill's solicitors showed him little respect. 'This is not' – so ran their covering letter – 'to be taken as an invitation by us to you to attend and appear at the Argument: indeed we are doubtful if you have any *locus standi*'†.[2] In fact the constitutional importance of the case, known as a 'relator action', required the intervention of the Attorney-General, Sir Frederick Smith, who, together with the Solicitor-General, Sir George Cave (both future Lord Chancellors), appeared on behalf of the Home Secretary.

The King v Sir Edgar Speyer and *The King v Sir Ernest Cassel*. On appeal as *The King, at the relation of Sir George Makgill, Bt v Speyer*.
†legal standing.

On specific instructions, Roskill made an unusual preliminary statement on behalf of his client. Unlike Cassel, Edgar had filed no evidence. Roskill explained his client's feeling that, having publicly offered to resign his privy councillorship, and having given his reasons for so doing, it would be paradoxical now to assert his right to it; but that having been directed by the Court to do so, he desired to comply by appearing through Counsel. Nevertheless, said Roskill, his client did not wish it to be thought that he was doing anything inconsistent with what he had offered in his letter to the Prime Minister.

This declaration could hardly be expected to make a favourable impression on the Bench. In effect Edgar was intimating that he did not care much one way or the other about the outcome of the case. The Lord Chief Justice quickly replied that the Court was concerned only to determine the point of law at issue and need not comment on Roskill's observation. The law was straightforward. Under the Naturalisation Act of 1870 a naturalised alien enjoyed the same rights as a natural-born British subject. The Act repealed by implication all previous legislation to the contrary, including Section 3 of the Act of Settlement. The appointment of Speyer and Cassel to the Privy Council was unimpeachable.

Having found in their favour, however, Lord Reading drew a significant distinction. Costs normally follow the event, but are a matter for the Court. While awarding costs to Cassel, the Lord Chief Justice ordered that Edgar should pay his own. On the face of it, the decision was uncontroversial, since Edgar had chosen not to engage in the action. In fact, it was intended as a deliberate slight. The reason, as Reading told Sir Almeric Fitzroy afterwards, was that while Cassel's conduct had been entirely correct, through his 'loyalty letter' in *The Times* 'attesting in earnest language his loyalty to the King and to the country of his adoption', Edgar's attitude, through his instructions to Counsel, was anything but. He had shown himself to be 'studiously disrespectful'. He had 'in substance told the King and the Privy Council to go hang'.[3] This lack, or apparent lack, of respect towards his membership of the Privy Council, would have lasting consequences.

On the dismissal of his action, Sir George Makgill appealed for donations, evidently with success, to enable him to take the case against Edgar to the Court of Appeal. He did not pursue his action against Cassel, perhaps because Cassel could point, as he had done in his 'loyalty letter', to the fact that all his closest relatives had enlisted in the King's service. The appeal, which was heard in July 1916, was rejected, the Court of Appeal confirming the decision of the High Court. For Makgill and the Anti-German Union, the outcome served to bring home 'the serious need for drastic reform of our naturalisation laws'.[4]

William Boosey's attempt to veto the performance of German music at the Queen's Hall as the insidious legacy of Sir Edgar Speyer was echoed a year later in the House of Commons by Sir Alfred Markham, who protested at the continuing predominance of German music under the baton of Sir Henry Wood. Both Newman and Wood had maintained a robust attitude from the first. A fortnight after war was declared, Newman riposted boldly to the cancellation, at Boosey's insistence, of a Wagner programme at the Queen's Hall. This, Newman made clear, was an unavoidable mishap dictated by 'outside pressure' brought to bear 'at the eleventh hour by the lessees of the Queen's Hall'. Beethoven, Brahms and Wagner remained staples of the repertoire, the Wagner evenings proving 'the chief success'[5] of the 1914 season. Pressure for a boycott revived with the sinking of the *Lusitania*, but Newman and Wood devised a clever compromise. They agreed that no music by living German composers would be played, since Germans would profit from the royalties. As for the classics, however, Wood roundly declared: 'There is no nationality in music'. 'To exclude a classic because it is German', he said, 'would be as unreasonable as to smash your piano because it is German'.[6] This was fairly unanswerable, and the 1915 season went ahead with a liberal repertoire of German classics.

But there was no let up in the pressure for official action against Edgar. Behind the scenes Conservative Central Office had encouraged the attacks by Leo Maxse on prominent Liberals of German origin.[7] The decision in the Makgill case was followed by questions in the House. At the end of July 1916, Major Newman MP asked the Prime Minister whether the Government would legislate to remove from the Privy Council any member not of British birth and to restore the law to what it was before 1870; and whether there was any reason to deny Sir Edgar Speyer's wish to be relieved both of his membership of the Privy Council and of his baronetcy. Asquith replied that no such legislation was contemplated. On the second point, he simply referred his questioner to the published correspondence between himself and Edgar, to the effect that the King had not been minded to grant Edgar's request. Apart from his own distaste for the agitation on the subject, doubtless the Prime Minister did not intend to enter into discussion of the legalities. As far as the baronetcy was concerned, the law appeared to be that the Crown could not accept the surrender of a hereditary dignity.

Four months later, on 6 December 1916, Asquith was ousted from the premiership by a Conservative-dominated coalition headed by Lloyd George and backed by the Northcliffe Press. That Edgar, though out of sight in America, was far from out of mind in London and had been neither forgiven nor forgotten, was immediately clear from press reaction. On the day that Asquith's Government fell, Northcliffe's *Evening News*, followed next morning by the *Daily Mail*, jubilant at the demise of 'the old gang', published a cartoon showing the new, combative Prime Minister, Lloyd George, in the cockpit of a fighter-plane, shooting down a zeppelin named 'Haldaneism'. In the gondola of the falling dirigible were Asquith, Grey and – Sir Edgar Speyer.

The Conservatives were not disposed to see Edgar let off with paper squibs. The 'Unionist War Committee' was a Conservative 'ginger group' strongly critical of Asquith's lacklustre leadership and his perceived softness towards 'the enemy within'. In late 1916, its 'Enemy Influence subcommittee' under Sir Edward Carson was busy considering the unsatisfactory outcome of the Makgill case. In January 1917, it formally demanded that legislation be enacted to bring about the disqualification of naturalised Germans from membership of the Privy Council.

The Clerk to the Privy Council, Sir Almeric Fitzroy, who was, as has been seen, an inveterate enemy of Edgar, scuttled busily behind the scenes, malign and venomous, intent on assisting in his downfall. In 1915 he had made a point of attending the Makgill case. The Court had directed that a copy of the *quo warranto* order be served on him as an interested party and at Lord Reading's invitation he even sat next to the judges. Three years later, in August 1918, with the approval of Lord Curzon, Lord President of the Council, he passed to the Home Office notes he had made of his conversation with Reading the day after the hearing. Fitzroy had elicited from the Lord Chief Justice opinions critical of Edgar's loyalty and tending to the conclusion that he should be removed from the Privy Council. His notes, Fitzroy thought, 'might be useful'[8] to the Home Secretary in determining, under the new Aliens Bill now before Parliament, whether to revoke Speyer's citizenship.

In the summer of 1918 the war still raged on unabated and had reached its culminating crisis. Russia was out. Italy and France were exhausted. America had barely entered the conflict. Victory and defeat lay in the balance. They would be decided where the war had begun – on the Western Front. The succession of massive offensives unleashed by Ludendorff in a final bid to reach Paris had smashed through the British Fifth Army, thrown the Allies back to Amiens and the Marne and had not yet been stemmed. None could foretell the outcome, but the stakes were desperately high.

How could these tremendous German advances in the fourth year of the war be explained? In London, Noel Pemberton Billing, MP, had one simple answer. Defending himself in person against a charge of criminal libel, Billing insisted that German agents in England had compiled a 'Black Book' containing the names of 47,000 Englishmen and women addicted to sexual perversions, who, under threat of exposure, had divulged valuable information to the enemy. Among those listed in this remarkable inventory, Billing, in open Court and to gasps from a packed public gallery, named Asquith, Margot Asquith, Haldane and even the trial judge! Acquitted by a credulous jury, Billing lost no time before rising in the House of Commons to renew the outcry against the remaining uninterned aliens with a question about 'the number of damned Germans that are running free about the country'.[9] The Speaker ruled the question out of order. Billing refused to desist. He was 'named' by the Speaker and forcibly removed from the Chamber by the Sergeant-at-Arms and four attendants.

The frenzied obsession with 'the enemy within' and the sinister machinations of a 'hidden hand' reached a peak. The Prime Minister himself, Lloyd George, gave voice to it ten days later, complaining in the Commons of anonymous letters he said he received from Germans 'crowing over' British setbacks:

> They are obviously written by Germans and the writers say they are Germans. Where are they? I feel that that sort of thing has got to be stopped.[10]

On 8 July, the *Evening News* announced on its front page: 'This is Enemy Alien Week'. Three days later, a huge demonstration, said to be the biggest since the war began, filled Trafalgar Square. Two large placards summed up the protesters' demands: 'A Clean Sweep' and 'Intern Them All'.[11] On hearing of this, the King was outraged. '"Intern them all," indeed!' he exclaimed to Margot Asquith. 'Then let them take me first! All my blood is German. My relations are German. Let me be interned before Cassel or Speyer'.[12]

The British Nationality and Status of Aliens Bill, discussion of which preoccupied Parliament in the second half of 1918, was the product of the public agitation that had raged throughout the war. Lord Charles Beresford, now raised to the peerage, was no less vocal a popular tribune in the Lords than in the Commons. 'What the public really wants', he declared, 'is that all naturalised subjects of enemy origin should have their naturalisation papers revoked'.[13] Ever alert to the demands of public opinion, Lloyd George, even at this critical juncture of the war, made it his business to put in an appearance when the Commons discussed the Bill. 'I myself', he declared, 'during the last few weeks, in spite of other urgent matters, have given consideration to it, because I regarded it as a matter of great concern affecting the prosecution of the war'.[14] How the elimination of naturalised Germans in Britain could affect the outcome of the tremendous struggle on the Western Front, the Prime Minister did not explain. Did he too believe in the influence of the 'hidden hand'? Or, more plausibly, did he seek, for political advantage, ostensibly to lend it credence?

The fury against Prince Louis of Battenberg and Sir Ernest Cassel, which had blazed a few years earlier, searing both its victims, had largely spent itself. Lord Sandhurst, for the Government, pleaded for Prince Louis, now anglicised as the Marquess of Milford Haven, and Cassel, exonerated by his family's war record, to be relieved of further obloquy. This left Edgar to face the brunt of the anti-German campaign as the Bill's most prominent target. In the Commons, Noel Pemberton Billing denounced the 'German Jew called Edgar Speyer, who is now working out the damnation of this country in America'.[15] A month later, on 29 July, Bonar Law, under intense pressure from his backbenchers, brought up the issue of Edgar's membership of the Privy Council before the War Cabinet. Chaired by Lloyd George, the War Cabinet agreed that once the Aliens Bill became law, Edgar's case would be referred to the Committee to be set up under it. Bonar Law informed the Commons accordingly the same evening (and Curzon the Lords three days later).

On 24 August another mass rally took place in Hyde Park. A monster petition, containing 1¼ million signatures and 'rolled up like a big drum',[16] was conveyed to 10 Downing Street on a lorry. It demanded the immediate internment of every German in the country. Behind the lorry, waving flags and bearing placards, a long, motley procession wound its tumultuous way through the West End: discharged servicemen, members of the Anti-German Union (now calling itself the British Empire Union), vigilantes still on the hunt for German spies, Trade Unionists, top-hatted City gents in frock-coats, their women-folk and other camp-followers. Lloyd George was not in Downing Street to receive the petition. When this became known to the demonstrators, now in Trafalgar Square, they held another mass meeting to express their disappointment in a resolution deploring the Government's failure to appreciate 'the deep national feeling' about 'the great peril of the enemy alien at large'. Every Member of Parliament should be asked whether or no he favoured 'the internment of all enemy aliens'.[17]

As the tide of war began, at long last, to turn gradually but unmistakably against Germany, so the anti-German temper at home continued to rise. Much of it was understandable. The Germans were in retreat on the Western Front, but they withdrew in good order and British troops paid heavily for every advance. Casualties were as heavy as at any time since 1914. On 10 October, even as the German Government, conscious that the war was lost, was sending out peace-missives to President Wilson, the Kingston to Holyhead mail-boat, the *Leinster*, was torpedoed in the Irish Sea, with the loss of 400 lives. 'Brutes they were when they began the war', the Foreign Secretary, the normally soft-spoken Balfour, said in the Commons, 'and, as far as we can judge, brutes they remain'.[18] Evidence emerged daily of wanton but deliberate destruction by the retreating Germans in France and Belgium and of maltreatment of the 60,000 British prisoners-of-war in German hands. To 'make Germany pay', both literally and metaphorically, became the keynote of a vocal public opinion.

The Prime Minister, intent on a general election to

renew the Coalition mandate, did not demur from the proposition that his Conservative allies would go to the polls on what C P Scott, editor of the *Manchester Guardian*, described to him as 'an orgy of anti-Germanism and the aliens hunt.'[19] Lloyd George himself was no fanatic. When asked what he would do with the mammoth petition unloaded at Downing Street, his secretary had replied, with a grin: 'The dustmen will have it'.[20] There must be limits to the 'smelling out' of aliens, Lloyd George warned the Commons. 'There are', he reminded them, 'few people in this country who are not of Teutonic origin. I'm not sure', he added, to laughter, 'that I am not the only survivor on the Treasury Bench who is not of alien origin.'[21] While Lloyd George himself might not personally go all the way with the hard men among his Tory allies, however, he was expediently ambivalent and far from unwilling to profit electorally from their zeal.

Within days of the Armistice, the temperature was further raised in Parliament. Lord Beresford observed, with some justice, that the new Aliens Act was passed 'in deference to public agitation and was not brought forward by the Government itself.'[22] Its purpose was to invest the Home Secretary with power to revoke certificates of naturalisation.

Under the Naturalisation Act of 1870 no such power existed: naturalisation, once granted, was permanent. The Act of 1914 allowed for revocation if the certificate had been obtained by fraud, but the Act of 1918 went far beyond this. The new Act authorised the Home Secretary to revoke a certificate of naturalisation on various stated grounds, notably disloyalty to the Crown 'by overt act or speech' or communicating or trading with the enemy, or where an individual's retention of his certificate would not be 'conducive to the public good'; and these were the heads under which charges would eventually be brought against Edgar. Such charges would be examined by a judicial committee, chaired by a High Court judge appointed by the Home Secretary in consultation with the Lord Chancellor. The Home Secretary, Sir George Cave, confirmed that if his certificate of naturalisation was revoked, 'Sir Edgar Speyer will cease to be a member of the Privy Council'.[23]

But suppose Edgar forestalled the Home Office and stole its thunder? For at this juncture Edgar did attempt to defuse the whole overheated issue in the most obvious way: by cable to Downing Street. Just as in his letter to Asquith three years before, so now: 'I once more, in a message to the then Prime Minister, Mr Lloyd George, tendered my resignation as a member of the Privy Council. To this message I received no reply'.[24] The authorities pondered the telegram. Downing Street passed it on to Buckingham Palace. The King was advised that it was a matter for his Ministers. The Home Office – particularly Sir John Pedder, the Permanent Under-Secretary with special responsibility for aliens – had its sights fixed on Edgar, determined that the new law should take its course and that an expectant public should not be baulked of its Roman holiday.

What evidence did the Home Office have against Edgar? A file on him was opened, but at this stage its contents were meagre. On 17 September 1918, Sir John

Pedder had written to Sir Eric Drummond, private secretary to the Foreign Secretary, Balfour:

My dear Drummond,
Under the British Nationality and Status of Aliens Act which was recently passed, the question of the revocation of Sir Edgar Speyer's certificate of naturalisation will be raised. As you probably know, a Committee of a judicial character has been appointed to consider such cases, and they are just beginning their operations. It is desirable in Sir Edgar's case to obtain all the available evidence for the guidance of the Committee. The enclosed memorandum contains a summary of the information at present in our possession. It is particularly desirable to obtain further evidence from America as to the relations between Sir Edgar Speyer and the New York House when he went to New York. Sir George Cave would be much obliged if Mr Balfour could obtain from America any further evidence bearing on the case, especially on the particular point mentioned.

The information which we have hitherto obtained from the other side up to the present is perhaps hardly adequate, as you will see from a private note which I also enclose. This is intended for your use only and not to be sent to New York.

We should like to have the further information as soon as possible. Mr Fisher Williams has been dealing with the case in the Home Office, and he would be able to give the Foreign Office any further particulars they require. Perhaps you would care to let him

see any dispatch in draft so that he can say whether it
covers the points on which information is desired.

Yours sincerely[25]

The 'private note' enclosed with the letter, a statement of everything known about Edgar's activities in
America, confirms that while the Home Office might
have reason to suspect him, it had no evidence whatever
on which to lay charges against him.

The decision to charge Edgar was thus taken long
before there was anything to charge him with. The Home
Office kept prodding and prying. It set enquiries afoot
on several fronts. It asked Scotland Yard about Edgar's
activities before his departure for America. Sir Basil
Thomson, head of CID and an assiduous wartime spy-
catcher, whose persistence had helped to bring Sir Roger
Casement to the scaffold, was asked whether the police
had any evidence of 'disloyal or disaffected act or speech'
or 'unlawful communication with the enemy' or association with any business which he knew would assist the
enemy. Special Branch had kept a file on Edgar since
1914. During the first year of the war it had received
numerous hostile reports, but having looked into them
at the time, it could find 'no evidence that Sir E Speyer
was doing anything to assist the enemy or against the
law of this country'.[26]

It was not a promising start for the authorities. A
minute of 29 October 1918 from Sir John Pedder, advis-
ing the Home Secretary on his reply to a Commons question on the progress of proceedings against Edgar,

confirmed that his case, when heard, would be 'on counts still to be settled'. Pedder observed:

> The case is a very difficult and important one, likely, I suppose, to be fought hard: and at present the evidence is by no means complete. It will take some time to work it up. Enquiries are being made in [the] USA.[27]

What, then, of Edgar's activities in America? In September 1918, a senior official had advised that 'before launching the case', the British Embassy at Washington 'should be pressed for any further evidence which they have'.[28] What evidence did they have? How had Edgar spent his time in the United States? In the summer of 1915, a few months after his arrival in New York, he had moved to Boston. He found it congenial, the nearest equivalent to an English town. Opinion there was pro-English. It was a literary and above all a musical centre. He spent most of his time there, going to Bar Harbor on the Maine coast for the summer months, and this became the pattern of his life.

He joined the St Botolph Club, meeting-place of the Boston literati, though he noticed that 'a great many members did not seem very keen to know me';[29] and he moved largely among musical friends and acquaintances, including the Dean of the Boston Conservatory. He attended concerts by the Boston Symphony Orchestra, and he got to know its celebrated German conductor, Dr Karl Muck. The Crown was to make much of this, and of his association with John Koren, treasurer of the St

Botolph Club, a man with a strong interest in music and the arts. Edgar's name appeared occasionally in the social columns of the newspapers, but he shunned publicity, gave no interviews and issued no statements. He was anxious to avoid controversy and he was annoyed when a report of the Makgill case appeared in the *Boston Journal*. Ostensibly his life was one of quiet retirement, centred upon music.

The British authorities thought otherwise. Since early in 1918, the Home Office had pressed the War Trade Intelligence Department and, through the Foreign Office, the British Embassy in Washington and the British Military Mission in New York, to expedite enquiries and produce results. The Home Office pursued several lines of enquiry. In particular it sought information on Edgar's 'attitude towards the pro-German activities' of Speyer & Co in New York, and 'how far knowledge of those activities can be brought home to him'[30] since his arrival in America. It was known that on his arrival in New York Edgar had used the firm's address as his own and that he had sent his own business cables from the offices of Speyer & Co. These, however, proved to be temporary arrangements and there was nothing unlawful in them. Had matters gone further?

A memorandum of August 1918 to the Home Secretary from John Fisher Williams, the Home Office official in charge of Edgar's file, went straight to the point. Did Edgar's activities fall within the ambit of the new legislation? 'The crucial question', wrote Fisher Williams

is whether or not after his arrival in America Sir

Edgar Speyer so far took part in the pro-German activities of the New York house ... as to bring himself within the terms of Section 7 of the B[ritish] N[ationality] & S[tatus] of A[liens] Act as now amended as having either 'shown himself by act or speech to be disaffected or disloyal' or by having 'unlawfully traded or communicated with the enemy or with the subject of an enemy state or ... have been engaged in or associated with any business which is to his knowledge carried on in such manner as to assist the enemy' in the war.[31]

When the United States entered the war in April 1917, James Speyer and Eduard Beit von Speyer had severed the connection with each other's House. Until then, Speyer & Co had continued as before to conduct the large-scale business with Germany for which they had been on the British blacklist since December 1915. Business had been carried on either through banks in neutral states or directly with German banks, including Speyer-Elissen, by means of coded messages designed to evade British monitoring of telegraphic and wireless communications. However hostile to British interests, this was something Speyer & Co were free to do as long as the United States remained neutral.

America once a belligerent, however, the American authorities, as well as the British, now turned their attention to Speyer & Co and James was called in for questioning. He complained vociferously about the blacklisting. 'The British are down on everything connected with me', he said, adding incautiously: 'I wish we were at war with some other people than the Germans'. Realising that he had gone too far, he tried to make out that he had in mind the Japanese, but the inference was 'unmistakable', his interlocutor noted. 'He referred to Great Britain', which he criticised repeatedly and with 'strong antagonism'.[32]

As for Edgar, Lord Chief Justice Reading, as has been seen, while ruling in his favour on the point of law in the Privy Council case in 1915, had ruled against him in the matter of costs. The day after giving judgment, Reading had encountered Sir Almeric Fitzroy, who asked whether now that Edgar appeared to be transacting business through the New York House, he ought to be removed from the Privy Council. Reading 'replied without hesitation: "Yes"'. He also assented to Fitzroy's suggestion that he, Reading, should press the point 'as strongly as possible'[33] on Prime Minister Asquith.

It so happened that from late 1915, by a wholly unforeseeable chain of events, the fortunes of war found both Edgar and Lord Reading on American soil. While Edgar's star was in free fall, however, Reading's had taken spectacular upward flight, the more remarkable in contrast to his situation not long before the war, when his reputation was still overshadowed by his prominent exposure in the Marconi scandal. Disgruntled Conservatives might continue to rake up the affair, but once the war began, Reading's unrivalled financial expertise and persuasive advocacy made him indispensable both to Asquith and to Lloyd George. In the autumn of 1915 Reading spent six weeks in the United States, not as Lord Chief Justice, but as head of an Anglo-French mission to negotiate American credits. In the course of meetings with American bankers, he told Fitzroy, James Speyer 'had moved heaven and earth to obtain an interview with him'; but the dexterous, diplomatic and now far more cautious Reading had taken care to avoid him. 'He knew him to be the tool, if not the spy, of Bernstorff, and that was enough for him'.[34]

Nor did Reading have anything to do with Edgar. Much had changed in the year since 1914, when the two fellow Liberals were on friendly terms and Edgar, then at the outset of his troubles, had written to thank Reading for 'your more than kind letter', for which Edgar expressed himself as 'touched' and 'very grateful'.[35] Having burned his fingers over Marconi, Reading was at pains to keep out of trouble; and if anyone spelled trouble now, that man was Edgar.

Three years later, Lloyd George was Prime Minister, and his faithful emissary Reading, now Earl of Reading, was Ambassador Extraordinary in Washington, where he first eclipsed and then replaced the actual ambassador. In the spring of 1918, at the supreme crisis of the war, Reading stood at the height of his authority with both the American and British Governments. It was then that, acting on instructions originating from the Home Office, he found himself looking into Edgar's activities in America. Then, on 6 April 1918, he dispatched in cipher the following cable to the Foreign Secretary, Balfour:

Personal
Confidential. I have received a letter from Sir Edgar

Speyer, informing me that he wishes to return to England on business matters, and asking to see me for the purpose of obtaining my advice. Please inform me whether you have any views on the subject of his proposed visit to me and his return to England. My inclination is against permitting visit to me: it might easily be misinterpreted.[36]

Reading's meaning was that if Edgar were known to have been received by the Ambassador it would go down badly in England. It was scarcely of less concern to Reading that such a meeting might reflect badly on himself.

In any event, the answer was no. Balfour replied four days later:

I share your view as to the undesirability of receiving a visit from the gentleman in question, and all idea of his return to this country should be discouraged.[37]

Reading put off successive requests by Edgar to see him, and Edgar gave up trying. Reading then took up the question of Edgar's legal standing in America. He learned from the State Department that, under a presidential proclamation, any person of German birth finding himself within the jurisdiction of the United States, even though a naturalised British subject, became under American law an enemy alien, liable to internment. The question, as Reading informed the Foreign Office in a 'personal telegram'[38], was whether Edgar was born in Germany. 'If this suits our views', he cabled slyly, 'would you let me know his birthplace'.[39] The Foreign Office, while mildly objecting on principle to any British citizen's being classified as an alien, commented: 'as to calling him an alien, we have no desire to protect Speyer'.[40] The lucky chance of Edgar's birth in New York spared him the humiliation of arrest and internment in the United States.

Even before America entered the war, the American intelligence services had extended their surveillance to Edgar. Enquiries began in 1916, during his summer sojourn in Maine. His friend, Karl Muck, noted contemptuously:

> A secret service fellow is loitering about here just now. He divides his attention between Sir Edgar Speyer (in Bar Harbor) and myself. Idiots.[41]

The reports of the secret service agents were of the cloak-and-dagger variety. The Home Office described them as 'rather melodramatic'. Detectives had burgled the New York apartment where Edgar's 'confidential secretary' lived. The secretary, they were told, had on occasion displayed symptoms of extreme nervousness. He had had to be sedated with bromo-seltzer, and had slept in his clothes 'with a revolver under his pillow'. They were not clear why. They thought he might have been attempting to blackmail Edgar. They had found a code, which, however, might have been a banking code. They heard tell of late-night conversations between Edgar and the secretary. They raided the Speyers' own apartment. They interviewed domestics. One domestic spoke of a scrapbook containing newspaper reports of U-boat sinkings. A housemaid told of 'a mysterious meeting' in 'Lady Speyer's boudoir', of conversations in German between the Speyers and miscellaneous visitors, said to include a German naval captain, a member of the Boston Symphony Orchestra and a man with the unlikely name of Guggengiggle. The same housemaid mentioned a piece of paper containing Chinese characters, whose disappearance appeared to alarm Leonora, of a 'black bag' belonging to Edgar and of Edgar's frequently burning papers. The agents hoped with the housemaid's assistance to secrete from the apartment several volumes of Edgar's poems, one of which was thought to glorify the Germans. The Americans concluded that from this 'muddled story it seems possible that some mysterious and curious things are going on'. The Home Office commented that 'very little so far seems to have come'[42] of it, and so worthless was this farrago of hearsay that no use was made of it at Edgar's trial.

Back in England, political considerations after the Armistice gave added impetus to the campaign to bring Edgar to account and brought his name back to public attention. The 'coupon' election of December 1918 returned the Lloyd George Coalition to power with a landslide majority, but still left the Prime Minister heading a mainly Conservative ministry, with an enlarged host of unruly Conservative backbenchers. 'George thinks he won the election', a Tory minister commented. 'Well, he didn't. It was the Tories that won the election, *and he will soon begin to find that out*'.[43] Asquith and his followers were routed at the polls. In his own constituency, which he had held for over 30 years, the former

Prime Minister confronted a placard reading: 'Asquith nearly lost you the War. Are you going to let him spoil the Peace?'[44]

At the hustings Lloyd George did what he could to whip up public expectations of a peace of reparation and retribution. In his notes for a key speech on 29 November he wrote: 'Deal at this meeting with all controversial matters'. 'War indemnity' headed his list of priorities, followed, as he promised his enthusiastic audience, by the 'exclusion from amongst us of a people who abused our hospitality to spy on us and plot against us'.[45] Prominent among his electoral slogans, together with the well-known promises to 'Make Germany Pay' and to 'Hang the Kaiser', was a pledge for the 'Expulsion of the Enemy Alien'.[46]

CHAPTER V

The Trial (i) *Two-penny-ha'penny transactions?*

This exceedingly unpleasant and repugnant investigation.

Sir Gordon Hewart, KC, Attorney-General, 17 October 1921

On 22 March 1919, the Home Office wrote to inform Edgar that the Home Secretary was considering revoking his certificate of naturalisation and had referred his case to the Committee of enquiry set up under the new Aliens Act. The Home Secretary himself, Edward Shortt, informed the House of Commons accordingly three days later. The announcement, long awaited, long promised and long delayed, was premature, however, since there were still no charges for the Committee to consider, a fact of which Shortt was keenly aware. The Foreign Office pressed the Washington embassy for evidence of Edgar's activities in America, and the *chargé d'affaires* gratifyingly reported that while a full dossier was not yet complete, the information available so far 'is not favourable to Speyer'.[1] Investigations continued on both sides of the Atlantic. Much later, the Chief Assistant Solicitor in the Treasury Solicitor's Department, the department responsible for giving legal advice to the Government, gave the game away when he ingenuously wrote that the purpose of the Home Office enquiry 'is to obtain the denaturalisation of Sir Edgar Speyer'.[2] But that had been clear from the beginning.

On 5 November 1919, Messrs Williamson Hill & Co, Edgar's solicitors, having received no particulars of any alleged charges, wrote to the Treasury Solicitor urging him, after a delay of almost eight months, 'either to withdraw any such charges or to deliver particulars of the same to us at once'. 'In a case of such gravity', they complained, 'the particulars must either be in your possession or the charges should never have been made at all'.[3] Three weeks later the Treasury Solicitor replied:

> The papers in this matter are now before Counsel, and I hope to be able to let you have particulars of the matters alleged against your client within such time as will permit of the case being heard at a reasonably early date next year.[4]

Charges were brought in February 1920. They related to Edgar's activities after he left England, and fell into two categories. The first category alleged that he had shown himself 'disloyal or disaffected' to the King by associating with pro-Germans in the United States. The second category alleged that, through his association with Speyer & Co, he had 'unlawfully traded or communicated with the enemy' or had been 'associated with business which, to his knowledge, assisted the enemy'.[5] Particulars of the second category of charges, drawn from sheafs of wartime telegrams intercepted in London, were not served on Edgar's lawyers until November 1920.

A year later, Edgar obtained from the Committee an order for evidence to be taken on commission in America, where testimony was duly gathered with a view to rebutting the charges relating to his activities there. Meanwhile the authorities in England redoubled their efforts in the search for evidence against him. Yet as late as August 1921, Henry Giveen, Junior Treasury Counsel, was sceptical whether the charges would stick. In a 'Preliminary Opinion' Giveen wrote: 'I have at present some doubts as to how far it may or may not be possible to establish the Crown's case'. Referring to the costs of evidence-taking in America, however, he concluded: 'Considerable expense has been already incurred, and it is desirable in view of this and also of the position of Sir Edgar Speyer and the notoriety which the case has already obtained, not lightly to abandon it'.[6]

Confident – for his lawyers so advised him – that the case against him would not hold up, Edgar returned to England in August 1921, after an absence of six years, to face the charges. This delay was not all of Edgar's making. Before 1914 a British subject could leave or enter the country without let or hindrance or even a passport; but the powers of the Home Office to interfere in private life had been greatly extended by successive variants of the Defence of the Realm Act, a statute popularly caricatured as the bossy governess-figure of 'Dora'. In the spring of 1918, as has been seen, the Foreign Secretary instructed Lord Reading, then Ambassador in

Washington, to discourage Edgar's attempts to return to England. Early in 1919 Edgar made a fresh application to the British authorities in America for his passport to be renewed, but, he noted, 'it was delayed from week to week'. He wrote half a dozen times. 'There was always some excuse made'.[7] Now, almost three years later, while the Home Office at last renewed his passport, it sought to curtail his travel plans.

Edgar wished to go to France, to meet his American lawyer who was holidaying there. He planned to visit his sister in Berlin and his now widowed brother-in-law Eduard in Frankfurt, neither of whom he had seen since before the war. He also hoped to spend some time at Karlsbad, where he had last taken the cure in May 1914. The Home Secretary did not object to his seeing his lawyer, but could see 'no reason for granting facilities to enable him to travel abroad for other purposes'. The Home Office did not want to be criticised for 'comforting and assisting a man whose certificate is being questioned'.[8] So much for any presumption of innocence. The Foreign Office, however, took a more enlightened view and Edgar's passport was endorsed accordingly.

On 17 October 1921, the three members of the Certificates of Naturalisation (Revocation) Committee, to give it its full title, took their seats in Court 5 of the Royal Courts of Justice to hear the case of Sir Edgar Speyer. Nominally a judicial enquiry held at the instigation of the Home Secretary under the Aliens Act, this was in reality a full-dress state trial, prepared for the Law Officers of the Crown by the Treasury Solicitors as agents

of the state in political prosecutions; and while the lawyers on both sides began by fastidiously shunning the
word 'charges' in favour of 'heads of enquiry', the Law
Officers deprecating the very idea that they were 'prose-
cutors in any sense at all',[9] this flummery was soon forgotten in the familiar ardour of adversarial contest. Both
sides referred openly to 'the Crown' and the Committee
was referred to as 'the Court'. The Committee was armed
with all the powers of the High Court, and though formally a 'witness', Edgar was as much on trial as if he
were in the dock.

To all intents and purposes, then, this was a criminal
trial, in which a guilty verdict would mean that Edgar
was liable to suffer one of the most formidable sanctions
available to the state: deprivation of citizenship – or, as it
is sometimes called, 'civil death'. The proceedings were
held in the King's Bench Division under the presidency
of a High Court judge, Mr Justice Salter; an elderly
County Court judge named Francis Radcliffe and Lord
Hambledon, a layman with a high reputation for public
spirit. Proceedings were held *in camera*.

The hearings had already begun when fresh evidence
against Edgar was introduced. After pertinacious
searches, the dusty shelves of the Admiralty archives had
yielded up their secrets in the shape of transcripts of
long-forgotten wireless messages, intercepted by Naval
Intelligence during the war. These finds were gold-dust
for the authorities, enabling fresh charges to be lodged as
late as 21 September, the evidence itself emerging piece-
meal and, as Edgar's Counsel complained, 'at the 59th
minute of the eleventh hour'.[10] These charges alleged

Mr Justice Salter
'However learned in law... reached unjust conclusions on insufficient evidence'. Edgar Speyer

Edgar's complicity in trading with the enemy before as well as after his departure for America.

The main charges against Edgar may be summarised as follows: that he had shown disloyalty during the war (1) by continuing to do business, directly or indirectly, with Germany, (2) by violating the censorship regulations, (3) by communicating with Germans and (4) by assisting Germans; (5) that he had befriended and assisted pro-Germans in America; and (6) that he had formed the intention of settling in Germany.

The case for the Crown was opened by the Attorney-General, Sir Gordon Hewart, and the Solicitor-General, Sir Ernest Pollock, soon to become, respectively, Lord Chief Justice and Master of the Rolls. They were assisted by Henry Giveen. Edgar was represented by two eminent KCs, Sir John Simon and John Henry Roskill. Roskill had appeared for him six years before in the Makgill case. Edgar's legal costs, consisting chiefly of his lawyers' fees, were said to exceed £20,000. Edgar was present throughout and gave evidence. He was cross-examined and re-examined. His other main witness was his junior partner in Speyer Bros, Gordon Leith.

For much of the hearing, the Attorney-General did not attend. He was needed at Downing Street, to assist in negotiations for a peace treaty with Ireland. His mastery of the facts in the Speyer case, however, suffered no diminution from his preoccupation with Irish issues and his opening cross-examination of Edgar was brutally efficient.

ATTORNEY-GENERAL: When was it that you decided to prefer British allegiance to German allegiance?

SIR EDGAR SPEYER: You mean when I became naturalised?

ATTORNEY-GENERAL: No. I am asking you of the state of mind, not of an overt fact like that.

SIR EDGAR SPEYER: I decided that about two years before I came to England.

ATTORNEY-GENERAL: That you preferred to be a British subject?

SIR EDGAR SPEYER: Yes.

ATTORNEY-GENERAL: You came to England when?

SIR EDGAR SPEYER: I came to England in 1887.

ATTORNEY-GENERAL: So that about the year 1885 you decided that it was preferable to be a British citizen?

SIR EDGAR SPEYER: Yes.

ATTORNEY-GENERAL: And you have remained of that mind ever since?

SIR EDGAR SPEYER: I have.

ATTORNEY-GENERAL: For example, during the late war did you ardently desire that England should succeed?

SIR EDGAR SPEYER: Yes.

ATTORNEY-GENERAL: And you ardently desired that Germany should fail?

SIR EDGAR SPEYER: Yes.

ATTORNEY-GENERAL: You never wavered in that at all?

SIR EDGAR SPEYER: No.

ATTORNEY-GENERAL: Were you throughout prepared to do whatever you could to bring about that result?

SIR EDGAR SPEYER: I was.

ATTORNEY-GENERAL: And to abstain from anything whatever which might conduce to the opposite result?

SIR EDGAR SPEYER: Yes.

ATTORNEY-GENERAL: You became a member of the Privy Council in the year 1909?

SIR EDGAR SPEYER: Yes.

ATTORNEY-GENERAL: Five years before the war; and you took the oath of a Privy Councillor?

SIR EDGAR SPEYER: I did.

ATTORNEY-GENERAL: ... Did you ever have the curiosity to read it?

SIR EDGAR SPEYER: Certainly.[11]

Hewart then read aloud two passages from the Privy Councillor's oath and invited Edgar to confirm that he had abided faithfully by his sworn obligations to the Crown.

The authorities, understandably, had always been deeply suspicious of Edgar's connections with Speyer & Co; and while it was not denied that he had resigned from the Frankfurt house on the declaration of war, the Crown alleged that he remained a further two months in partnership with James in the New York house, which continued to do business with Germany and of which Eduard Beit von Speyer was also a partner. This, said the Crown, was in contravention of the Royal Proclamation of 5 August 1914, which declared trading with the enemy to be illegal. It was only after a second proclamation on 9 September that Edgar resigned from Speyer & Co, and only then, the Crown contended, after a further month's delay. Sir Gordon Hewart pressed this home:

ATTORNEY-GENERAL: ...You knew, did you not, that transactions, joint dealings, between London, New York and Frankfurt, would be illegal after the war [began]?

SIR EDGAR SPEYER: Yes, certainly, if Frankfurt was in it.

ATTORNEY-GENERAL: You knew, did you not, that unless active steps were taken to prevent them, they would be probable, they would be likely to happen?

SIR EDGAR SPEYER: Yes.

ATTORNEY-GENERAL: ...As to the illegality of joint dealings after the war [began] between London, Frankfurt and New York, let me remind you of the letter which was sent to the New York Stock Exchange, dated 5 October 1914.

The Attorney-General then read aloud a letter of 5 October 1914 from James Speyer to the Secretary of the New York Stock Exchange, in which he gave formal notice that following the Royal Proclamation of 9 September 'it becomes necessary' that Edgar sever his connection with Speyer & Co.

ATTORNEY-GENERAL: You observe the word 'necessary' – 'it becomes necessary'?

SIR EDGAR SPEYER: Yes.

ATTORNEY-GENERAL: I suggest to you that you took that step reluctantly and at the last moment. Is that right?

SIR EDGAR SPEYER: I do not think so.

ATTORNEY-GENERAL: Let us see. There was put in [evidence] a letter dated 18 September 1914 from your Solicitor to you?

SIR EDGAR SPEYER: Yes.

ATTORNEY-GENERAL: …You had a long conference with your Solicitor upon the point, did you not, before that step was taken?

SIR EDGAR SPEYER: Yes, we certainly had.

ATTORNEY-GENERAL: Did not you suggest to him various alternatives that might be considered to enable you to continue carrying on your business?

SIR EDGAR SPEYER: What I said to him was this – please advise me what I ought to do.

ATTORNEY-GENERAL: Let us see what he wrote in reply …'Dear Sir Edgar, I have been thinking over the question you put to me as to whether it would be necessary for you to retire from Messrs Speyer & Co if they do no further business throughout the war with anyone in the German Empire' …Now, pausing there for a moment, I ask you, that was the question you had put to him?

SIR EDGAR SPEYER: Evidently.[12]

The Solicitor had advised: 'I think that strictly speaking you should not continue in the firm', but suggested applying to the Board of Trade for a special licence to remain in partnership. The Proclamation made provision for such licences but Edgar decided not to apply. Quite apart from 'the practical certainty that it would have been refused', it would, he said, in the prevailing climate of opinion, 'have made a very bad impression if I had asked for it'. [13]

The cross-examination continued.

ATTORNEY-GENERAL: …In other words, to put it quite plainly, I fear I must be plain—

SIR EDGAR SPEYER: I hope you are.

ATTORNEY-GENERAL: It was no spontaneous act upon your part which caused you to retire from the New York House… It was the Proclamation against trading with the enemy and the legal advice you got about it that compelled you to do so, was it not?

SIR EDGAR SPEYER: No doubt it was.

At this point Mr Justice Salter intervened.

MR JUSTICE SALTER: You remained a partner in Speyer & Co for about two months after the war broke out, from the beginning of August to the beginning of October. That is about right, is it not?

SIR EDGAR SPEYER: Yes.

MR JUSTICE SALTER: During that time, I suppose, New York was trading with Frankfurt and Berlin in its usual way?

SIR EDGAR SPEYER: I expect they did.

MR JUSTICE SALTER: You so understood. You were during that time a co-partner in the firm with Mr Beit von Speyer?

SIR EDGAR SPEYER: Yes.

MR JUSTICE SALTER: And you and he were taking your share in the profits of that trading?

SIR EDGAR SPEYER: It was arranged, of course. I did not share in the profits when I left the firm.

MR JUSTICE SALTER: I am speaking of the time before you left. So long as you remained a partner in that firm, you and he had your share of the profits, of course?

SIR EDGAR SPEYER: Yes, we certainly should have had them.

MR JUSTICE SALTER: Did it occur to you at the time as being undesirable that you should be a partner with an enemy, sharing profits with him?

SIR EDGAR SPEYER: I almost immediately began to consult my lawyer as to what were the best steps to take, but he took some time considering the matter. Of course, the chief motive in my reluctance, on which such stress is laid, was this. Our credit was at stake, and I was reluctant to leave Speyer & Co at a time when our liabilities were very heavy… and I was very much afraid of the effect it might have on our general financial position. Therefore I had to act with great circumspection. The idea of profit never entered my head. It was simply a question of protecting the credit of the English House.

The Attorney-General seized his cue.

ATTORNEY-GENERAL: In other words, your own financial interests?

SIR EDGAR SPEYER: If you want to put it so, yes.[14]

The Committee's findings on this charge were damning. It held that, acting 'with obvious reluctance and on compulsion', Edgar had 'preferred his private financial interests to the prompt discharge of his duty to the State'. Such censure reflected the Committee's view of the 'considerable time'[15] during which he remained a partner in a firm that traded with Germany, and in partnership with a German, and its assumption that he shared in the profits of such trade.

Edgar described the findings as 'amazing'.[16] In the first place, as he rightly claimed, the first Proclamation, issued the day after war was declared, had given rise to much uncertainty. War had come as a bolt from the blue. Its precise legal implications were far from clear, even in official circles. The world of business and finance was taken wholly aback. The Government had no thought of impeding British trade: rather it hoped that the blockade of Germany might open up German markets to British entrepreneurs. A Liberal Government was not minded to curtail freedom of trade more than appeared strictly necessary, still less to abolish it by proclamation. As late as November 1914, in a speech at the Lord Mayor's Banquet, Churchill famously invoked the slogan 'business as usual'[17] to indicate the tenor of Government policy. The Proclamation itself was ambiguous: while forbidding transactions with persons resident in Germany, it placed no restriction on trade with German firms in neutral countries, a distinction which required a ruling by the Lord Chief Justice to clarify.[18]

In these circumstances, business with Speyer & Co appeared to remain lawful, and, as Edgar protested, not he alone but 'thousands of loyal British subjects' retained 'with perfect propriety'[19] their connections with American concerns which traded with Germany. In this he was staunchly supported by his English partners. In a letter to the press in his defence, they confirmed the lack of clarity at the start of the war 'as to the correct action for those with international banking interests'. 'Any businessman', they wrote, who recalled those days, would 'appreciate the difficulties and perplexities with which Sir Edgar was confronted.' To the Committee's findings, they declared, 'we attach little importance'.[20] The legal position remained obscure until the proclamation of 9 September. Even then, its application was a matter on which Edgar was surely entitled to seek legal advice? The Committee's cut-and-dried verdict reflected the stricter view on trading with the enemy which evolved in subsequent wartime legislation rather than the vague and less sharply defined view prevailing in 1914.

Edgar was also justified in maintaining that his delay in resigning from Speyer & Co was of one month's duration, not two. Given the Committee's harsh strictures, the point was important but appears to have escaped his own Counsel as well as the Committee. The sequence of events was as follows. The solicitor's advice was dated 18 September 1914, seven working days after the second Proclamation. Four days later, on 22 September, Edgar wrote to James to communicate his resignation from Speyer & Co, *backdated to September 9*, the date of the Proclamation. He wrote promptly and with no obvious sign of 'reluctance':

> I am advised by my lawyers that under the Proclama-
> tion of September 9th last, my continued partnership
> in your firm has become illegal, and I therefore give
> you notice that my partnership in your firm termi-
> nated *from that date* [my emphasis –AL].[21]

Cables to America could not be relied on. The letter of severance went by sea. It would take about ten days and would therefore reach New York around 2 October. James notified the secretary of the New York Stock Exchange on 5 October. However long it took for Edgar's letter to arrive made no difference to its retrospective effect. So much for the Committee's finding of 'considerable delay'.

As for the profits which Edgar allegedly drew from Speyer & Co across two months, the Committee's censure was misplaced. At most, it could only have related to a single month. In fact, Edgar insisted that since the declaration of war he had 'derived no profit from this partnership' and he might well protest that 'there was no proof whatever' to support the Committee's 'gratuitous conclusion'.[22] The Committee's withering condemnation, which received prominent coverage in the press, was baseless and unjust.

The next charge related to April and May 1915, before Edgar left for America. It alleged indirect trading with the enemy in the course of currency dealings. Such dealings were potentially lucrative in wartime because of unusually violent fluctuations in currency values, and provided they were not conducted directly with the enemy and were not intended to benefit him, they were not *prima facie* unlawful. Edgar encouraged Speyer Bros to participate in them, though they played a minor role in the firm's business overall. In some of these transactions the principals were the New York house and Teixeira de Mattos of Amsterdam: Speyer Bros acted as a clearing-house, receiving and paying out moneys as agent. In other transactions Speyer Bros traded jointly with Teixeira, and the New York firm was the clearing-house.

These were the charges that were laid three weeks before the Enquiry opened, the evidence being lodged after proceedings had begun. At the time, according to Edgar, 'these new charges... appeared so trivial and so readily susceptible to explanation that... Counsel decided to proceed in spite of the disadvantage that they were first sprung at the hearing'.[23] Sir John Simon argued that Speyer Bros' operations had been 'quite legitimate exchange transactions... but which may, incidentally and unintentionally, touch Germany'. 'That', he contended, 'is not trading with the enemy'.[24]

The case for the Crown was that the real object of the transactions was to transmit funds to Germany. Teixeira traded regularly with Germany, and the Committee held that 'as an expert financier', Edgar 'should have known', and did know, that the transactions would enable Germany to acquire Dutch florins and other currencies of use in purchasing war materials from neutral states. 'Knowing this', the Committee concluded, 'he shared the profits of such trading.'[25] When Speyer Bros acted as agent for the New York and Amsterdam banks, their commission was 1/16 of the profit on the transaction; when Speyer Bros were joint speculators with Teixeira, the total profit accruing to the two firms from April to June 1915 was £1,920. Of Speyer Bros' £960 half share of this, Edgar's personal entitlement was some £300 – in Sir John Simon's words 'a comparatively trumpery profit'.[26]

Under cross-examination Edgar let his temper show.

'I had much more important things to do', he said, 'than to worry about than these two-penny-ha'penny Amsterdam transactions, which did not interest me in the least'.[27] The Crown professed to be shocked at the vehemence of this expression. Invited to explain himself, Edgar pointed to his overriding concern to alleviate the problems of Speyer Bros' responsibility to British investors in the failing railway companies, involving many tens of thousands of pounds:

> The transactions that mattered to me were transactions that concerned British investors, that is, the Manila Railway, the Underground Railway, the Brazil Railway, the San Francisco Railway, the M[issouri], K[ansas] and T[exas] Railway. Those were important things compared with which these were two-penny-ha'penny transactions.[28]

The Committee was not impressed by Edgar's explanation. It concluded as follows:

> We are clearly of opinion that Sir Edgar Speyer engaged in these transactions with Teixeira with knowledge that they involved benefit to individual Germans and assistance to the enemy in the war.[29]

Edgar denounced these findings as 'grotesque' and 'not sustained by a vestige of proof'. He was bitterly ironic about the £300 by which he was supposed to have benefited – 'Just think of the incentive here disclosed for disloyalty on my part!'[30] He maintained that the charge of trading with the enemy had 'failed utterly at the hearing and has no foundation whatever'. In transmitting funds to neutral countries, including Spain, Sweden and Switzerland, as well as Holland, through banks known to trade with Germany, 'Speyer Brothers did no more than was done by loyal British bankers'. If the Government wished to prohibit such transactions, 'they should have said so'. On the contrary, to their knowledge, 'they were participated in by every great British banking house throughout the war without protest by the Government'.[31]

His partners fully supported him. Gordon Leith was recalled to testify that Lazard Bros, Seligmans, Rothschilds and the London County Westminster and Parr's Bank among others all took part in exchange dealings. Such traffic had not been considered a crime at the time, Leith told the Committee, 'and I do not consider it a crime today'.[32] To have enquired of Teixeira de Mattos as to the ultimate destination of moneys sent to them for currency purchases would have been wholly contrary to banking practice, even in wartime. It was not even certain that specie which found its way to Germany would actually remain there rather than moving on in the course of further currency deals. Such advantage as would accrue to Germany if the chain of transactions did end there was, so to speak, adventitious. If the aim of Speyer & Co had been to transfer money from New York to Berlin, they could have sent it directly: there was no need to go through Speyer Bros at all. Edgar's partners protested that if the dealings held against him were to be classed as 'trading with the enemy', then 'hardly a bank or banking house in London can escape condemnation'. They went further:

> Sir Edgar has nothing to reproach himself with, since all the transactions of his firm were with neutral countries, viz, Holland and America; and to suggest that he, personally, engaged in this particular class of business with the knowledge that these transactions would 'involve benefit' to individual Germans and assist the enemy in the war is, in our opinion, a grave injustice to him.[33]

It had been no less in Britain's interest than in Germany's to acquire neutral currencies – for the purchase of munitions in the United States, iron ore in Sweden and Spain and dairy products in Holland. As Leith told the Committee, 'if exchange transactions had been forbidden, the world trade would have stopped, so we should have been in trouble too.'[34] The Government even connived at the sale of British goods to Germany through neutrals under cover of undertakings, more or less spurious, by the latter, that they would not sell on. British exports to Germany through Holland were notorious. They ranged from cocoa to cotton and included such wartime essentials as rubber, nickel and aviation fuel. British cement for the formidable German blockhouses reached the western front by the same channel. As for those detected in this trade, some were treated leniently while the law reached out to those with German connections or German names. Bringing this charge against Edgar was selective.[35]

Five of the 14 pages of the Committee's Report –
more than one third – related to evasion of the censorship to which all communications leaving or entering
the British Isles were subject. The day after war broke
out, Britain severed Germany's submarine cables in the
English Channel, after which almost all telegraphic communication between Germany and America passed
through London and came under the scrutiny of the War
Office censor. Wireless messages were the province of
the Admiralty censor. From November 1915 mails conveyed by sea on neutral vessels were liable to interception under the stop-and-search procedures of the Royal
Navy.

There was no doubt that Edgar did evade the Censor. He made no attempt to deny it and he admitted at
the hearing that it was wrong. Speyer Bros was an enterprise operating in both hemispheres, dependent for its
daily transactions on telegraphic contact and already fac-
ing daunting financial challenges on the eve of war. Its
business came to a virtual standstill when the authorities
took control of the means of communication. From the
moment of his arrival in New York, Edgar found that
cables which he sent to Speyer Bros in London and
cables to him from Speyer Bros were not getting through.
He was in error, understandably so, in attributing this to
the malice of the British authorities against him personally, and aimed at bringing about the ruin of his House.

Speyer Bros had indeed been singled out for special
surveillance, but for reasons of which Edgar was com-
pletely unaware. Once again his brother James had been
playing him false. Since April 1915, Speyer Bros had

been used as an innocent intermediary in exchange dealings between Speyer & Co and Germany. Speyer & Co acted in collusion with Teixeira. Disguised in a code privy to the New York and Amsterdam houses, messages from Speyer & Co to Teixeira, passing by cable through Speyer Bros in London, concealed important transactions with Germany. The code was broken by British intelligence. The authorities, including Asquith and Sir Edward Grey, were informed and the Home Secretary placed an embargo on the receipt and transmission of cables by Speyer Bros, pending investigation. It was further to the discovery of these transactions that Speyer & Co was placed on the Black List. Speyer Bros, and Edgar in particular, came under suspicion of complicity in the subterfuge practised on them by James, but were cleared by a Home Office enquiry in June 1915. The Committee of Enquiry, however, reopened the whole issue.

Ignorant in 1915 of the stratagem played on him by James week after week behind his back, Edgar had reacted indignantly to the blocking of his communications, as he told the Committee:

> I was very much incensed about it, and inasmuch as my telegrams were all telegrams which concerned British interests, and very important British interests – urgent telegrams dealing with financial affairs of Companies in which a great many British people were interested; I thought it was of the utmost importance that they should go through, when I thought it was unwarranted that they did not.[36]

To Edgar in New York, trying to resume his normal business activities, the Censor's interference was 'quite intolerable' and 'absolutely inexcusable'.[37] He had contrived to evade it by addressing cables to his British partners at their home addresses and requesting them to cable him through American intermediaries, adding openly 'and I do not mind if the Censor should open this letter, if he reads it, as we cable nothing that he need not see'.[38]

When his partners demurred at this attempt to flout the regulations, Edgar responded forthrightly:

> There is nothing that I cable, or that I ask you to cable, which need not be seen by the Government or anybody in authority. I simply want to attend to my business, and if for some reason of red tape or unfounded suspicion, some official chooses to hold up our cables, I consider I am justified to try and get a message through if I can through some friend. I do not mind anybody reading this, or anything else. I consider I am within my rights. If the Censor will tell us, or me, why he holds up our cables, we shall know where we are; but in the presence of what I consider unjustifiable proceedings I personally shall not hesitate to try and get in communication with my firm, if that is at all possible, by what you call 'indirect means'. [39]

The Attorney-General picked this up. 'Are not you really saying', he put it to Edgar, 'that in this matter you regard yourself as above the law?'[40]

Edgar's Counsel strove to repair the damage.

'What was your object in doing this?' Roskill asked him.

SIR EDGAR SPEYER: Simply to get my telegrams through.

MR ROSKILL: Had you anything to conceal?

SIR EDGAR SPEYER: Nothing whatever.

MR ROSKILL: Were those telegrams solely in relation to matters and securities that you had issued?

SIR EDGAR SPEYER: Absolutely.

Mr Justice Salter, who clearly attached high importance to strict and unquestioning compliance with wartime regulations, and was not disposed to take a lenient view of any kind of evasion, seized on the point.

MR JUSTICE SALTER: If you sent a message in such a way that the authorities would not know that it was to Speyer Bros, and therefore would not look at it, would that in your opinion be an evasion of their wishes?

SIR EDGAR SPEYER: Yes, I think it would be an evasion, but a different kind of evasion than changing the names in the telegrams themselves. The message was *en clair*; there was nothing in the telegram which was changed.[41]

Mr Justice Salter took a grave view of what he described as Edgar's 'repeated and systematic attempts' both to evade the censor and 'to seduce his English partners to do the same'[42] and of his recalcitrance in justifying his conduct:

It does not appear to have occurred to his mind that the duty of a loyal subject in a time of great national danger and anxiety is not to impede and defeat the efforts of the Government, but to cooperate with them, even at some personal inconvenience.[43]

Sir John Simon pleaded that evading the Censor, however reprehensible, 'is not treachery. It is not disloyal. It is not a reason for losing citizenship'.[44] It was essentially no more culpable, Sir John suggested, than drinking out of hours in breach of wartime licensing regulations. The Committee was not amused and it was not persuaded. Mr Justice Salter was adamant in holding Edgar's conduct to be 'inconsistent with any feeling of loyalty to His Majesty or of affection for the British cause'.[45]

At intervals during the war, and in undeniable breach of the censorship, Edgar was in correspondence with Eduard and Lucie at Frankfurt, and through Eduard with his sister in Berlin. In March 1915, this had come to the notice of the Home Office, which requested an assurance that all correspondence with 'persons in enemy country'[46] would cease. Edgar gave the assurance. The correspondence nevertheless resumed after he left England. His letters touched on business as well as family matters. Edgar and Eduard had exchanged complaints about the interference of the British censorship and the disagreeable sense of someone looking over their shoulders.

Mr Justice Salter regarded with great severity such exchanges, in which Edgar had indulged – the Committee noted reprovingly – as though Eduard were 'a fellow-subject or a neutral'.[47] The fact that Eduard was his brother-in-law, that Lucie was his own sister, did not strike Mr Justice Salter as mitigating circumstances. Sir John Simon again pleaded that, after all, the Aliens Act 'does not say that a man is to lose his British nationality because he tries to get past the Censor'.[48] Mr Justice Salter was adamant:

> This correspondence is plainly unlawful communication with the subject of an enemy State during the war. It was in breach of Sir Edgar Speyer's oath as a Privy Councillor and in flagrant and habitual violation of his personal undertaking. In our opinion, such a correspondence would have been impossible to any loyal British subject.[49]

In one particular the Committee appeared willing to make allowances. Several of Edgar's communications to Eduard took the form of requests to make small payments to distressed friends in Germany and Austria. Dr Weiss was a Karlsbad masseur who had ministered to Edgar before the war. 'I was in poor health', Edgar explained, 'and this man restored me to health… I felt that I could not let a poor man to whom I owed so much, starve'. Hugo Becker, cellist, composer and professor of music at Berlin, had been a close friend of Edgar since their schooldays. 'The idea', said Edgar, 'that one of my oldest friends should be in want was very painful to me'. Becker's sister-in-law, an artist named Tilly Struth, 'also a very old friend of mine', was in a similar plight and 'not in very good health'.[50] In Vienna another friend, a Frau

Hossner, was destitute. Before charges were brought in relation to these persons, Sir Basil Thomson of Special Branch had been asked to verify through the German police that Dr Weiss, Professor Becker, Frau Struth and Frau Hossner really existed and were not code-names.

These friends had confidently deposited their savings with Speyer Bros before the war, with no suspicion that they might one day be at risk. War once declared, Edgar scrupulously reported these holdings, as he was obliged to do, to the Custodian of Enemy Property, and they were duly sequestrated. Finding themselves suffering real hardship, the friends appealed to Eduard in Frankfurt for advances against what were after all their own funds. Eduard had raised the matter with Edgar, who approved the advances. Edgar conceded that his action was unlawful, and the Committee agreed that 'if the matter stood alone, we should attach no great importance to it'.[51] In the circumstances, however, Edgar's acts of friendship were counted against him as part of his record of illicit communication with the enemy.

CHAPTER VI

The Trial (ii) *Facing the music*

Zwei Seelen wohnen, ach! in meiner Brust.

'Two souls, alas, dwell within my breast' Goethe, *Faust*

W hat was the tenor of Edgar's social life in the United States? Who were his wartime associates? For these too fell to be scrutinised by the Committee. A disproportionate amount of time, based on evidence supplied by the American intelligence services, was devoted to the consideration of two charges which in the end were dismissed as nugatory. First, a temporary loan by Edgar of $5,000 to a would-be purchaser of the *Boston Journal*, who had latched onto Edgar while he was holidaying in Maine in April 1917. Much energy was expended at the hearing to discussing articles in the *Boston Journal* said by the Crown to be suspect because of a contributing reporter, thought to be anti-British. There was nothing in the charge. The Committee concluded that Edgar had advanced the loan out of 'good nature'[1] to a professional scrounger.

Then there was Edgar's association with one John Koren, one of his Boston acquaintances, treasurer of the

St Botolph Club, a professor of statistics appointed by President Wilson to represent America on the International Prisons Commission. In 1916 Edgar contributed another $5,000 in order to subsidise a European fact-finding mission by Koren, which included a visit to Germany, though not to England. From the Crown's point of view there were some suspicious circumstances to the trip, including a social call by Koren on Edgar's sister in Berlin and his cousin, Arthur von Gwinner. The main purpose of the trip was to ascertain how far there was support for the setting up of a neutral commission after the war to investigate its causes, a project of which Edgar approved. After exhaustive examination, the Committee concluded that it would be unsafe to draw 'any inference of disloyalty or disaffection'[2] from these facts.

A friendship to which the Crown attached far more significance was that which Edgar formed with the celebrated German conductor Karl Muck, whom Edgar described with justice as 'one of the greatest conductors in the world'.[3] Appointed director of the Berlin State Opera by the Kaiser before the war and celebrated for his renderings of Wagner – his gramophone recordings are still prized – Muck had conducted regularly at Bayreuth. At the time of the Speyers' arrival in America in 1915, he had been conductor of the Boston Symphony Orchestra for three years. Not only was the Boston Symphony Orchestra, in Edgar's words, 'the finest orchestra in the United States', but 'there was nobody in the United States who, in the musical world, was more highly regarded than Dr Muck'.[4]

Edgar came to know Muck soon after he settled in

Boston, as he could hardly have failed to do. As he said, 'everyone knew Dr Muck in Boston'.[5] Leonora herself had made her concert début with the Boston Symphony Orchestra at the age of 18 and had made Muck's acquaintance later in London when he conducted at Covent Garden. Austere and somewhat humourless, Muck was 'a highly cultivated man', Edgar told the Committee, a classical scholar who 'read Greek and Latin in his leisure time'.[6] The Speyers and Dr and Frau Muck struck up a friendship. They went for drives together and regularly received one another. They enjoyed discussing music and they enjoyed performing it. There were concert-parties, at which Leonora played to Muck's accompaniment. What could be more natural than their association? But at a time of growing tension between America and Germany it was almost bound to give rise to suspicion, especially since, as Edgar agreed, 'we always spoke German'.[7]

'What were Dr Muck's sympathies in the war?' Edgar was asked by Roskill.

'They were undoubtedly pro-German', he replied.

'You knew that?'

'Yes, I did.'

'Was there any other reason than your interest in music that made you associate with that man?'

'None whatsoever'.

They had tacitly agreed to avoid the subject of the war. Edgar explained:

> When we first met, naturally the war cropped up once or twice; but I made it clear to him, and I will

Karl Muck

'One of the greatest conductors in the world'. Edgar Speyer

say this for him, that he was not keen on discussing it with me and we did not discuss it.[8]

Sir John Simon sought clarification. 'What did you make clear to him?' he asked.

Edgar explained that they had disagreed about submarine warfare. Muck held it to be a legitimate reaction to the British blockade and the interception of merchant ships by the Royal Navy. 'I pointed out to him that this was not the case, that one was taking life and the other was simply interference with trade, and he then said, "Here speaks the Englishman"'. In any case, said Edgar, Muck preferred 'to talk about music and art. He wanted to get away from'[9] the subject of the war.

Off the coast of Maine lies the fashionable island townlet of Bar Harbor. Set among wooded mountains, it was the holiday resort of several well-known American families – an American equivalent of Overstrand – and it was here that Edgar and Leonora came annually for the summer. Bar Harbor was also a focus of musical life, 'a kind of Mecca', said Edgar, 'where everybody went to hear music ... a unique gathering of eminent musicians',[10] which included Kreisler and Paderewski. It boasted a splendid neo-classical concert hall, prominently situated on a pine-clad hillside. In 1917 Edgar had taken for the summer the modestly named Birnam Cottage, in fact a large Italian-style mansion. Other participants in the annual musical pilgrimage to Bar Harbor rented accommodation five miles away at another picturesque locality, Seal Harbor.

In June 1917 Karl Muck was thinking of renting a

cottage at Seal Harbor. America and Germany had been at war for three months. Muck had not been interned, for technically he was a citizen of Switzerland, but the letting-agent hesitated to let to a foreigner who made no secret of his pro-German convictions. At this point Edgar and Leonora intervened. They were keen to secure Muck as a near neighbour for the season. 'We were very anxious that Dr Muck should join the musical coterie there', Edgar told the Committee. 'His being there made a tremendous difference to the life of the neighbour-hood'.[11] They determined to bring their influence to bear. They drove to Seal Harbor and descended on the estate agent. They assured him that Dr Muck was Swiss, not German. Eventually the deal was clinched. Edgar invited the Mucks over to Bar Harbor for a celebratory dinner at Birnham Cottage. The *Boston Sunday Globe* described them as 'guests of honour'[12] at the Speyers'. The Crown sought to throw suspicion on Edgar's role in this episode, but Sir John Simon submitted:

> If it be a reproach that a man who is a British subject and who is interested in music should want to have one of the great musicians near him during the sum-mer in the musical circle, so be it.[13]

With America at war, Bar Harbor was rife with the kind of rumours that had shrouded Overstrand in 1914. Dr Muck's cottage was said to conceal traces of a radio transmitter, in fact parts of a wireless installed by a for-mer tenant, a radio-ham. Intelligence agents kept watch on the Speyers and the Mucks. They reported small-town rumours of signalling to ships at sea from the island's mountain-tops, of boats putting out from the shore to rendezvous with German submarines and the handing over of papers.

In the autumn of 1917 the name of Karl Muck suddenly achieved nation-wide notoriety in the United States. It was widely but falsely reported that he had refused to conduct 'The Star-Spangled Banner' at a public concert in Providence, Rhode Island. He had in fact been instructed not to perform it; but the story, scooped by the *Providence Daily Journal*, was syndicated from coast to coast, and publication of Muck's opinions in a subsequent interview with that paper did nothing to give the lie to it. Like Robert Newman in 1914, Muck boldly defended the universality of music. 'Art is a thing by itself', he declared, 'and not related to any particular nation or group'. So far so good; but it would have been wiser had he not added, referring to what was now the American national anthem: 'It would be a gross mistake, a violation of artistic taste and principles' for the Boston Symphony Orchestra 'to play patriotic airs'. He concluded, according to the *Providence Daily Journal*: 'To ask us to play "The Star-Spangled Banner" is embarrassing. It is almost impertinent... The public has no right to demand it.'[14]

Worse was to come. It turned out that Muck was conducting a torrid extra-marital intrigue. A safe deposit box containing a cache of his love-letters was broken into by the authorities, and these *billets-doux* revealed as much his devotion to the German cause as to his *inamorata*. He defended unreservedly the sinking of the

Lusitania. He wrote in contemptuous and abusive terms of America and its leaders, including the President, of his scorn for the tuxedoed and bejewelled society audiences before whom he performed and of a day of reckoning for the United States. He was known to be in regular contact with the German consul in Boston and the ambassador, Count Bernstorff. He was thought to have links with German agents. He was suspected of complicity in plots to sabotage American railways and factories. No charges were ever brought against him but in April 1918 he was interned in a camp for enemy aliens and subsequently deported.

Edgar denied any previous knowledge of Muck's alleged pro-German activities. When he learned of them, he professed himself 'absolutely dumbfounded'.

MR ROSKILL: Did he ever make the slightest, even tentative, approach to you in the matter of any pro-German act of his?
SIR EDGAR SPEYER: Never. [15]

Sir John Simon strove once more to convey sympathetically to the Committee the character of Edgar's relationship with Muck from his client's perspective:

> He was in retreat. He endeavoured to get such comfort and consolation as he could from what is the great artistic passion of his life, music. He found himself in the association of a number of musicians and undoubtedly was a good deal in their company.

Sir John emphatically repudiated 'the suggestion that the communications which he was holding and the friendships he was making were communications and were friendships which could possibly be regarded as indicative of disloyalty or treachery'.[16]

There was no evidence that Edgar knew Muck to be suspected of being a German agent, and this the Committee accepted; but he knew that Muck was an outspoken pro-German, and that, for the Crown, was enough. On these grounds the Solicitor-General, Sir Ernest Pollock, submitted that he 'can have done this country no good by that association'.[17] As a British subject in the United States, let alone a baronet and Privy Councillor, it behoved him to be especially scrupulous as to how his conduct might appear in American eyes. The Solicitor-General instanced the reaction of the *Providence Daily Journal*, which he put in evidence. 'Dr Muck', this newspaper informed its readers when breaking the story of 'The Star-Spangled Banner', 'has been one of the active heads of German propaganda in Boston, and the constant companion of Sir Edgar Speyer'.[18] On the basis of such evidence, Pollock invited the Committee to conclude that Edgar had shown himself 'disaffected and disloyal' as charged under the Aliens Act:

> He may have been fond of Karl Muck's music and musical genius; but in looking at what Sir Edgar Speyer has done, and what it was his duty to do, I say we have proved fully that he has associated himself with a man who was of German interest and German sympathies and in doing that, he committed a breach

of the duty which is laid upon him and referred to in the Act.[19]

The Committee agreed, and condemned Edgar outright and categorically:

> We think that this frequent and friendly intercourse with an avowed enemy of his country would have been repugnant to any loyal subject… We think that he should have known – he should have felt – that his open and friendly intimacy with a well known enemy of his country could not fail to be prejudicial to the British cause in the United States. [20]

Of all the charges levelled against Edgar one of the most damning arose from a letter to him from Eduard. The letter was discovered when a neutral vessel bound for America was stopped by the Royal Navy and the mail searched. The letter, dated 26 January 1916, was in response to a request from Edgar in which he asked Eduard to make certain enquiries of Arthur von Gwinner. Gwinner, who was Edgar's cousin by marriage, was a man of great consequence in Germany, a leading Berlin financier and a director of Germany's leading bank, the Deutsche Bank, with which Speyer Bros had done business before the war. Gwinner had been instrumental in financing the Berlin-Baghdad railway, for which the Kaiser had ennobled him and raised him to the Prussian Upper House. It appeared from Eduard's letter that Edgar contemplated settling in Germany in the event of a German victory and had sought Gwinner's advice as to a position in finance in Berlin. In a further letter to Edgar in March, Eduard confirmed that he had asked Gwinner what Edgar 'could do in Berlin if he came back after the war'.[21]

This was undeniably evidence of the most damaging character. When the Crown put it to him that in seeking Gwinner's advice 'you could not have got, if you had desired it, a more competent person upon the question of what would be your financial prospects in Berlin',[22] Edgar could not but agree. He denied, however, the imputation placed upon the correspondence. He agreed that Eduard had interpreted his intention in the same way as had the Crown, but he maintained that this was a complete misunderstanding of his true intention. At a time of depression, in virtual exile in America, he had indeed sought Gwinner's advice. His enquiries had been aimed, however, not at the possibility of taking up a position in Berlin, but of settling in the Tyrol or Italy, where, he said, he aspired to a life of retirement given over to literary pursuits.

This certainly seemed a tall story. 'What on earth was the value of Mr von Gwinner's advice as to whether you could settle down in Italy?' the Crown asked sceptically. 'To me of very great value',[23] replied Edgar. 'Gwinner', he explained, 'is a man who, in addition to being a very prominent man of business, is keenly interested in art and literature'.[24] He had sought Gwinner's advice, he said, not as a 'man of business' but as a relative and close friend who shared his artistic and aesthetic interests, a man of wide erudition and cultivated tastes. Was this, as the Committee found, partly from Speyer's 'own demeanour as a witness',[25] pure fantasy? Or could he have meant it? Certainly Edgar had a taste for versification. Several of his letters to Eduard included copies of his poems. As for Gwinner, he was known to be a man of unusually broad culture who quoted Shakespeare and Molière as readily as Goethe.

The Committee rejected Edgar's explanation and found that his intentions were as alleged. It is difficult to fault their conclusion. Edgar's original letter to Eduard was never produced. After the trial, Edgar submitted another letter, claiming that it was the original even though it was dated five months before Eduard's; Mr Justice Salter considered this proposition 'quite absurd'[26] and dismissed the evidence of the letter as utterly implausible.

The inherent unlikelihood of Edgar's explanation was brought out by a further piece of evidence. In the same envelope as Eduard's original letter was a second letter, from Eduard's wife, Lucie, Edgar's sister. This letter, also dated January 1916, was written at a time when the Central Powers were masters of the Balkans. The Allies had just abandoned the Dardanelles. Serbia lay crushed beneath the heel of the Austro-German and Bulgarian forces. Her defeated army was in full retreat. The Bulgarians had captured the strategic town of Nish, which brought the Berlin to Constantinople section of the Berlin-Baghdad railway under complete German control. Lucie's letter contained a cutting from a German newspaper, marked 'for Edgar', reporting a triumphant speech from Nish by the Kaiser after reviewing Bulgarian troops.

Lucie's letter was itself exultant. 'Our military situation,' she wrote, is 'excellent and wonderful'.[27] When the Allies evacuated Gallipoli, she and Eduard had had the house festooned with bunting. The Crown argued that Lucie would never have written to Edgar in such terms had she not felt certain that he would welcome it. It was consistent, as the Attorney-General put it to Edgar, with the belief on her part that 'camouflage apart, you were really a devoted German and ardently desired the success of the German arms and the defeat and humiliation, if it might be, of England'.[28]

Would Eduard, the Attorney-General asked, have entertained even the possibility of Edgar's settling in Berlin after the war, 'if Eduard really thought that Sir Edgar was a patriotic Englishman'?[29] The conclusion seems irresistible: not only had Edgar contemplated the possibility of a German victory – he could not be blamed for that — but he had also thought about what his own position would be in that eventually, and had put out feelers in Berlin. On these grounds the Committee found that

> Sir Edgar Speyer had ceased to entertain any feeling of loyalty to His Majesty or affection for this country, and that he desired (at least in the event of a German victory) to substitute for his British citizenship a German allegiance and association.[30]

It was not an unreasonable conclusion. Perhaps it was the only tenable one. A British subject cannot entertain a contingent loyalty, an allegiance which shifts with the fortunes of war. He is either for or against his adoptive country. Allegiance is a state of mind and heart, and as such is as much a fact as any other, equally susceptible of forensic determination.

And yet, precisely in Edgar's case, the Committee's verdict, even if legally correct, may not have been the whole picture. A man in Edgar's situation might well, as a matter of fact, entertain dual or divided loyalties. It was natural, it was inevitable for him to speculate on what would become of him if Germany won. He had, at that time, no desire to remain indefinitely in America. America had been a temporary place of refuge, not his permanent residence, nor even, as will be seen, except in a strictly legal sense, his domicile of choice. In his mind, England, however ill she had requited him, remained his homeland; but was it conceivable that he, Leonora and the children could resume life in an England defeated and perhaps occupied by the Germans? What future could there be for him, returning, as would inevitably be said, on the heels of a victorious German army? All that he had endured before would be as nothing compared to what he would inevitably encounter in those circumstances. Yet how serious and above all how lasting was the intention he formed to settle in Germany? Was it a fixed and settled intention or had it gone any further than an enquiry? If his intention was serious, it was not enduring, to judge by what he said and did later.

Whatever weight should be given to the rest of the evidence against Edgar, much, in retrospect, hangs on the letters from Eduard and Lucie. They may be said to be the pivot of the whole case. Was it so certain that, as the Committee held, he 'had ceased to entertain any... affection for this country'? Other facts speak in his favour: the pro-British sentiments he expressed to Muck, the good deeds which, as will be seen, he continued to perform for British friends in 1917 and the greater part of 1918, when Britain's prospects of survival were bleak. Above all, the Committee's finding was wholly inconsistent with his repeated efforts to obtain permission to return to England in the spring of 1918.

'The real question', said Sir John Simon, in his final submission to the Committee, 'is a question of motive'.[31]

> The important thing at each stage is to say: What light does this really throw on the final issue? Is there something which is anti-British, pro-German, something which, if not actually treacherous, at any rate is warmly resentful of the whole British cause and warmly adhering to the enemy? That is the real thing.[32]

Sir John pleaded for leniency for Edgar: 'Whatever his shortcomings may be, I submit that he ought not to receive the fearful condemnation which an adverse decision in a report of your Committee would involve.'[33]

The last word, however, was with the Crown. Proceedings ended on 7 November 1921 after almost 11 days of testimony and argument. Judgment was delivered in the form of a Report submitted by the Committee to the Home Secretary on 28 November and published as a parliamentary White Paper on 6 January 1922.

Of the nine formal charges laid against Edgar, three

were dismissed and one was upheld with mitigating factors. But the Committee concluded, with 'no doubt whatever':

(1) That Sir Edgar Speyer has shown himself by act and speech disaffected and disloyal to His Majesty;
(2) That Sir Edgar Speyer, during a war in which His Majesty was engaged, unlawfully communicated with subjects of an enemy state and associated with business, which was to his knowledge carried on in such manner as to assist the enemy in such war.[34]

Edgar returned to America immediately after the hearings, apparently confident that he would be vindicated. On learning the result, he asked for a re-hearing, mainly on the grounds that some at least of the Committee's conclusions were unsupported by the evidence. He sought leave to introduce further evidence in rebuttal. He would call Eduard and James to testify in his favour.

Inevitably the request was refused. Mr Justice Salter pointed out, not unreasonably, that Edgar could at any time have called further witnesses. If necessary an adjournment would have been granted. He had chosen not to. Even if Eduard and James had testified, Mr Justice Salter observed crushingly to the Home Secretary, 'the conviction which I formed during the hearing would not have been altered'.[35] The case was closed, and, the Home Office confirmed, 'cannot be reopened'.[36] 'Autolycus' in *The Sunday Times* made sneering reference to Edgar's 'bombarding the authorities... for rescission of the verdict', and a Cabinet Minister, Sir Robert Horne, made a classical witticism at his expense: *dum spiro, spero*.*[37]

In a letter of protest, released to the press, Edgar challenged the authorities to publish the full evidence on which the findings were based. He defied 'any fair-minded man'[38] to justify them. The challenge might sound heroic: but in fact the Home Office, after some debate, agreed that he was free, if he wished, to publish the documents himself. The authorities doubted that many would be tempted to scrutinise the voluminous mass of papers or that, if they did, it would convince them that the verdict was wrong.

Was Edgar fairly tried and were the charges against him brought home? Sir John Simon went to the heart of the matter when he invited the Committee to reject the contention that 'in no genuine sense was he other than his country's enemy and his country's enemy's friend. That is the real question'.[39]

A brief retrospect may be permissible to assist the reader to decide that question for himself or herself. From this retrospect two charges are omitted which have been shown to be unfounded but to which the Committee attached great importance: Edgar's alleged delay in resigning from Speyer & Co and his alleged drawing of profits from the company. Leaving these aside, let it be allowed, for the sake of argument, that the Committee's principal findings of fact were justified. What did they add up to? In sum, they amount to this:

------

*'I keep on hoping as long as there is breath in me', a punning reference to Edgar's surname.

(1) that Speyer Bros, like other British banks in the first year of the war, had dealt in a number of currency transactions, a by-product of which, to Edgar's knowledge, accrued to Germany's benefit;

(2) that Edgar had repeatedly and openly evaded the censorship despite a personal undertaking not to do so;

(3) that he had associated openly in America with Karl Muck, a known pro-German;

(4) that he had maintained a correspondence on business as well as family matters with 'the enemy' in the person of his brother-in-law; and

(5) that he had at one point formed the intention to settle in Germany if Germany won the war.

How far can these findings, singly or in aggregate, be said to justify the Committee's conclusions of disaffection and disloyalty?

The temptation should be guarded against of transposing today's standards on those of a century ago. After so terrible a war, narrowly won and at such cost, anti-German feeling remained understandably high. Yet the peaks of hysteria had passed. The war had ended three years before. The autumn of 1921 was not May 1915 when, as Kipling wrote, the English began to hate; or the summer of 1918, when that hate became an epidemic. Moreover, the Committee was a court of law. Whatever animosities might continue to rage outside, its function was to act judicially.

The Committee's proceedings partook of both enquiry and trial. It was inquisitorial and accusatorial.

This enabled and indeed obliged the chairman to intervene more often and more actively than in a conventional trial. Mr Justice Salter's interventions were persistent, pertinent, and penetrating, and they were invariably on the side of the Crown. The impression of his attitude throughout is of hostility. Judge Ratcliffe and Lord Hambledon sat mute: they were book-ends. It is not to impugn the integrity of Edgar's judges to observe that a different tribunal, or, to be frank, a different chairman, with a different scale of values, might have reached a different verdict. Nor is it irrelevant to note that all three members of the Committee were Conservatives, and that until his appointment to the Bench in 1917, Mr Justice Salter had for 20 years been MP for the Basingstoke division of Hampshire.

The Committee's final conclusion, which flowed from their other findings, was that the continuance of Edgar's certificate of naturalisation was 'not conducive to the public good'. 'On this point', said their Report, 'we can feel no doubt'.[40] Invited to reconsider the Committee's findings when Edgar submitted further evidence, Mr Justic Salter informed the Home Secretary: 'So far as I am concerned, I do not desire to alter a word in the Report.'[41]

'Not conducive to the public good' – the expression dates back several centuries – was the formulaic test laid down in the Aliens Act, 1918. To this day it remains the test in deciding whether or not an alien should be deported. Under the Aliens Act of 1918 the test was additional to, not merely, as the Committee held, consequent on, the findings of fact: it was required to be demonstrated that '*in any case* [my emphasis – AL] the continuance of the certificate [of naturalisation] is not conducive to the public good'. Did the Committee's findings, assuming them to be more or less correct, justify or lead of necessity to the conclusion reached? Was this really an exercise of judicial discretion or was the decision in essence political? Here it seems fair to question the Committee's judgment. That Edgar had not lived up to the high honour of a Privy Councillor may be admitted; but the question – at least the question before the Committee – was not whether his conduct made him unfit to remain a Privy Councillor but whether it warranted his disenfranchisement as a British citizen. Proof of his pre-war munificence and numerous acts of generosity during and after the war was presented in court – his lawyers made sure of that, even against Edgar's own inclination. The Crown played down such evidence. Generosity in a wealthy man might be taken for granted, said the Attorney-General, adding: 'We are not concerned in this case with the musical or charitable gifts of Sir Edgar Speyer, but with his conduct, and with his real sympathy.'[42] But were not 'musical or charitable gifts' valid examples of his 'conduct' and relevant evidence of 'his real sympathy'?

Mr Justice Salter confirmed that generosity was largely irrelevant. Perhaps he was right in the sense that the Committee's task was to establish the truth of the facts alleged by the Crown and to report on them; but was it not also its duty, in determining whether the continuance of Edgar's certificate of naturalisation was 'conducive to the public good', to consider and evaluate his record *as a whole* and decide whether *as a whole* it amounted to disloyalty?

Consider this portion of Roskill's examination-in-chief, aimed at eliciting from a patently reluctant Edgar details of his assistance to Englishmen and women during the war:

MR ROSKILL: Again, in defiance of your own wishes, I must ask you... First of all Mrs C, who had a son fighting for this country–

SIR EDGAR SPEYER (to Mr Justice Salter): My Lord, is it necessary that the name should be handed in? I only want to protect my friends, that is all.

MR JUSTICE SALTER: It is quite right that these things should be mentioned, not because generosity is of any materiality at all, but helping British subjects might be useful.

MR ROSKILL: Who is Mrs C, you know whom I mean?

SIR EDGAR SPEYER: Yes.

MR ROSKILL: Is she a lady whose son was fighting in the British Army?

SIR EDGAR SPEYER: Yes.

MR ROSKILL: Was she the widow of one of your oldest friends here?

SIR EDGAR SPEYER: She is.

MR ROSKILL: A very well known English gentleman and hunting man?

SIR EDGAR SPEYER: Yes.

MR ROSKILL: Did you take over her securities for a sum of over £6,000?

SIR EDGAR SPEYER: I did.

MR ROSKILL: At a time when they showed a depreciation of 80 per cent, which they still show?

SIR EDGAR SPEYER: Yes…

MR ROSKILL: The Queen's Hall Orchestra Endowment Fund had suffered severe losses in its investment?

SIR EDGAR SPEYER: It had.

MR ROSKILL: Was that a Fund to provide the members of the orchestra with pensions?

SIR EDGAR SPEYER: It was to provide payment when they left. It was not exactly a pension fund. It was not big enough for that.

MR ROSKILL: Did you pay the Fund £2,500 in order to take over from them depreciated securities worth £1,900?

SIR EDGAR SPEYER: If it is stated so.

MR ROSKILL: Were these particulars got out by Mr Greene, your secretary?

SIR EDGAR SPEYER: Yes.

MR ROSKILL: The fund, I believe, was originated by a payment from you of £500, and you gave an annual subscription of £100 to it?

SIR EDGAR SPEYER: I suppose so, if it is stated there.

MR ROSKILL: You have had in your firm for many years an Employees' Benevolent and Pensions Fund, which was also invested in securities?

SIR EDGAR SPEYER: Yes.

MR ROSKILL: Did you make up the depreciation in those securities in the month of June, 1920, by a gift of £10,000?

SIR EDGAR SPEYER: I did.

MR ROSKILL: To enable the distributions to be increased?

SIR EDGAR SPEYER: Yes.

MR ROSKILL: I come now to D, an English lady whose depreciated securities were £460, taken over by you in September 1919 for a payment of £600.

SIR EDGAR SPEYER: I daresay. I really do not remember these things.

MR ROSKILL: You have had these extracted?

SIR EDGAR SPEYER: Yes. I am sure they are all correct.

MR ROSKILL: Extracted at your Solicitor's request and at your Counsel's insistence?

SIR EDGAR SPEYER: Yes.

MR ROSKILL: Then Mr X. Is Mr X a friend in bad circumstances, and did you help him by giving him £1,000 a year from 1914 to 1919 to enable him to keep up his insurance policy?

SIR EDGAR SPEYER: I did.

MR ROSKILL: … Without going through them in detail, did you give over the whole of the war years some 16 friends in this country an average of £250 a year to recoup them for loss of interest on falling investments?

SIR EDGAR SPEYER: If my Secretary says that, I must have done that.

MR ROSKILL: Your chef was killed in the war?

SIR EDGAR SPEYER: And I sent his widow something.

MR ROSKILL: You sent his widow 3,000 francs?

SIR EDGAR SPEYER: Yes.

Giveen interjected for the Crown: 'Are all these after the war?' Roskill replied: 'Yes, they are all after the war'. Mr Justice Salter intervened to clarify: 'You mean after the beginning of the war?', to which Roskill assented, but Salter observed: 'Some were after the end of the war', to which Roskill replied: 'Yes, but none of them before the war'.[43]

All this was to no avail. The reader who has had the patience to follow these interchanges cannot fail to have noted the extent of Edgar's generosity to British citizens during the war. He might be thought to have done his 'bit', but Mr Justice Salter's comments, brief but suggestive, confirm that they had no influence with him. As for Edgar's more than 20 years of good works before the war, far from being weighed in the balance, they too counted for nothing. The Committee's Report dismissed them in a single sentence.

It is true that the Committee was bound by its own precedents. In 15 other cases referred to it by the Home Office 15 naturalised aliens had their citizenship revoked. The Committee stressed that it must measure Edgar's case against verdicts passed on smaller fry and not treat with any less severity 'the case of a man in high position, who is not only a subject but a servant of His Majesty'.[44] Those other cases too were heard *in camera*. Their particulars were not divulged and comparisons are not possible.

Under Section 7 of the Aliens Act, the Committee's decision took the form of a report to the Home Secretary, Edward Shortt, to whom responsibility for the final issue now passed. Sir John Pedder, the influential Home Office lawyer with special responsibility for aliens, was not slow to proffer his opinion. He advised Shortt that revocation of Edgar's citizenship was 'almost automatic'. The

Home Secretary, wrote Pedder, had 'practically no choice. He must revoke if satisfied as to disloyalty, and he could not, except for very strong reasons and with great difficulty, fail to be so satisfied... On this report', he concluded, 'the certificate must be revoked'.[45]

This was begging the question. The Committee had confined itself strictly to the allegations presented to it. It had signally, almost ostentatiously, failed to take any account of Edgar's long record of public and charitable munificence. It was open to Shortt – one is tempted to say it was his duty – to call for evidence of that record and to review the case as a whole before determining that for Edgar to retain British nationality was 'not conducive to the public good'. Shortt was not obliged, as Pedder urged, to rubber-stamp the Committee's recommendation. On the contrary, he was bound, in the exercise of his discretion, to form an independent judgment, to make up his own mind. This is clear from the debate in Parliament on the Aliens Act. Rejecting a proposed amendment that would have allowed for appeal to the High Court, the previous Home Secretary, Sir George Cave, had pointed out that under the Act the procedure was two-tiered and contained its own built-in safeguard by way of what was in effect an automatic appeal to the Home Secretary from the Committee's findings. He stressed that the final decision lay with the Home Secretary and that: 'The act is the act of the Secretary of State, and not of the Committee.'[46]

The Committee's Report was forwarded to the Home Office on 28 November 1921.[47] On 30 November Pedder drafted his advice for Shortt's consideration. Shortt was a

Liberal and a lawyer. Until lately he had held judicial office as a recorder. As Home Secretary he was said to be 'somewhat indolent in the routine work of the office and in detail'.[48] Be that as it may, on 1 December he signed an order under the Aliens Act directing that Edgar cease to be a British national. The order reproduced verbatim the conclusions of the Committee, by which Shortt pronounced himself 'satisfied'.[49] The order was of immediate effect. Edgar's comment was brief and bitter: 'the Home Secretary simply dared not give me the vindication to which I was entitled.'[50]

The Committee's report said nothing about Leonora or the children. Nor could it have done. Against them, of course, no charges had ever been brought. No shred of evidence, at least against the children, could be offered. The Aliens Act left that decision too in the hands of the Home Secretary. Since Leonora was American-born and had acquired British nationality only by marriage, there was no difficulty about including her in the revocation order. 'It is the general practice', Pedder confirmed, 'when a certificate is revoked, to deprive the wife also if possible of British nationality, so as to avoid her being of a different nationality from that of her husband'.[51] Few tears were shed for Leonora, for she was thought to have courted the stigma by her unconcealed contempt for English attitudes; and had the Home Secretary not revoked her nationality, loyalty to Edgar would no doubt have impelled her to repudiate it anyway.

Leonora's fate having been decided, the question was whether the sins of the father, if sins they were, should be visited on his three teenage daughters. Some qualms were expressed. All three were true-born British subjects. Their right to British citizenship was indefeasible at Common Law. The usual practice in such cases was to spare the children, 'unless', as Pedder wrote, 'in special cases it is desirable to eradicate the British nationality of the whole family'. Pedder evidently thought it was desirable. He noted that under the Act 'the whole family may be ousted at once'.[52] His colleague, Oscar Dowson, assistant legal adviser to the Home Office, disagreed. In the absence of compelling reasons, it was, he remonstrated, 'at least unsatisfactory' to deprive them of it by the use of statutory powers. 'On the whole', he concluded, 'I am inclined to think they should *not* be included in the Order for revocation'.[53]

The Home Secretary, on Pedder's advice, decided otherwise. Pedder, while professing to share Dowson's 'great reluctance' to deprive the children of their nationality 'by means of naturalisation machinery', concluded: 'I think it ought to be done here and I think it is in the best interests of the daughters', since otherwise 'they remain fixed willy nilly with British nationality while their parents are deprived of it.' Pedder felt that 'the whole family would prefer to be cast out together'.[54] The supposition was reasonable. The metaphor, suggestive of scapegoats, was apt.

CHAPTER VII

Retrospect: *Which of us was to blame?*

Suddenly fluttered a wing,
Sounded a voice, the same,
Somebody spoke your name:
Oh, the remembering!

Sounded a voice, the same,
Song of the heart's green spring,
Oh, the remembering:
Which of us was to blame?

Leonora Speyer, 'Suddenly', 1920

When we began this fight, we had clean hands – are
they clean now? What's gentility worth if it can't
stand fire?

John Galsworthy, *The Skin Game*, 1920

'I shall never forget nor forgive the treatment I have received. This may not be a fine sentiment but it is the true one at any rate',[1] Edgar wrote to Bernard Shaw in June 1915, shortly after his arrival in America. This feeling of powerful resentment and injustice was fuelled

Sir Edgar Speyer, Lady Speyer and Percy Grainger as 'The Unholy Family' on 'The Flight into Egypt' (Sir Philip Burne-Jones, 1915)

by his treatment by the British authorities across the next six years. It re-emerged when he testified before the Committee, as was noted by Oscar Dowson, assistant legal adviser to the Home Office, who was present during Edgar's cross-examination: 'He was evidently suffering from a strong sense of personal grievance at the treatment he had received since the beginning of the war at the hands of his country of adoption.' Dowson's overall impression of Edgar was perceptive, and – significantly – it differed from that of Mr Justice Salter. 'It is evident', wrote Dowson, 'that he had no *intention* to injure the interests of this country during the war... On all essential points Sir E[dgar] Speyer's conduct was loyal'.[2]

The Committee's report was released at the beginning of January 1922. The quality newspapers reproduced it in full, *The Times* under the heading 'Speyer Report Revelations'.[3] The press as a whole had a field day and revelled in Edgar's downfall. The *Pall Mall Gazette*, which before the war had hailed him as a Mr Cheeryble, headed its report 'The Unmasked Hun'.[4] The *National Review* exulted in the 'pleasant surprise' vouchsafed to the public by the detection of 'this snake in the grass'.[5] The *Daily Mail* referred to 'acts of flagrant disloyalty during the war' and 'deals that helped Germany.[6] A *Times* editorial, headed 'Sir Edgar Speyer', observed that Edgar was lucky to have had his naturalisation revoked. Had he remained a British subject, he might have faced the capital charge of treason for 'aiding and abetting the King's enemies'[7] in time of war. The *Daily Express* complained: 'Traitor Still a Baronet.'[8]

For seven years, from 1914 to 1921, many forces in society had been set in motion against Edgar. Stirred up by the war from the murky depths there emerged on the frothy surface of public life the delusional demagogues, the Beresfords, Bottomleys* and Billings, with their spymania and obsession with the machinations of a 'hidden hand'. Their vapourings were propelled, like poison-gas, by a powerful and sometimes irresponsible press. At the

---

*In May 1922, five months after the Speyer hearings, Bottomley was tried before Mr Justice Salter at the Old Bailey and convicted on 23 counts of fraudulent conversion. The judge sentenced him to seven years' penal servitude.

height of the vendetta in May 1915 a Liberal raged against 'the foul Northcliffe pogrom of people with German names'.[9] 'The *Morning Post* took the palm',[10] Edgar told the Committee; but the right-wing press as a whole was baying at his heels, echoing or inciting public and parliamentary opinion, while street processions and the rioting London mob hooted and vented their insensate fury on his head.

Deployed against him at one time or another were the principal organs of state: the Home Office under successive Home Secretaries, Scotland Yard and various branches of the intelligence service at home and overseas, the Board of Trade, the War Office, the Foreign Office and diplomatic services, the Law Officers of the Crown and the judiciary: all intent on bringing him to book.

Behind it all lay what? Envy of Edgar's wealth and prominence, dislike and suspicion of his political influence, fears and suspicions fired by the visceral resentments of war: justified fear of Germany as a powerful, resourceful and ruthless enemy, suspicion that Germans in England must feel the call of their homeland and would not shrink from obeying it. Edgar did nothing to demonstrate that he was above those suspicions, rather he fed them by his long silence and then confirmed them in the eyes of many with his letter to Asquith. Scapegoats were needed and Edgar fitted the part.

On receiving the Home Secretary's decision, Edgar was required to surrender his certificate of naturalisation to the Home Office, to be scored through and marked 'revoked'. Having ceased to be a British subject, he was no longer eligible, under the Act of Settlement 1701, to be of the Privy Council. Sir Almeric Fitzroy did not conceal his glee at the prospect of 'his expulsion from the Privy Council'. He prepared with long-anticipated relish for the formalities that would remove Edgar's name from the roll, 'a step I have long since pressed upon the attention of the authorities'.[11]

The King, in whose name this was done, took no pleasure in kicking a man when he was down. Now that the unpleasant duty was forced on him, he hoped that it might be done with a minimum of fuss. Fitzroy explained to the King's Private Secretary, Lord Stamfordham, that following the precedent of George III, notably in the case of Charles James Fox, the King might, depending on his sense of personal outrage, choose to strike out Edgar's name with his own hand. Stamfordham reported the King's aversion to 'anything so personal, and, if I may say so, theatrical'.[12] Of the squalid little ceremony at Buckingham Palace in which Edgar's name was duly expunged, Fitzroy noted unctuously that it was 'hailed with satisfaction by everyone present'.[13] These included the Home Secretary, Edward Shortt, and Sir Robert Horne, who had made the Latin quip at Edgar's expense. Fitzroy regretted only the apparent impossibility of divesting Edgar of his baronetcy, but took comfort in the thought that he had no male heirs to pass it on to.

Even literature played its part in the vendetta. It has been suggested that in his classic spy-thriller of 1915, *The Thirty-Nine Steps*, John Buchan may have had Edgar in mind in the character of Appleton, the German agent.

Certainly in the persons of Sir Hermann and Lady Gurtner, E F Benson cast Edgar and Leonora as the melodramatic villains of his novel *Robin Linnett*, set in 1914.
Benson portrays Sir Hermann, privy to secret information in July 1914, purchasing shares simultaneously in
Vickers and Krupps, and includes such unlikely touches
as the young Gurtner children singing *Die Wacht am
Rhein* at bedtime. A dozen years later, Benson evidently
thought better of this unkind travesty, for he produced a
far more sympathetic account of the true story in *As We
Are*, published in 1932 shortly after Edgar's death. Yet
even Benson assumed that the sentence pronounced on
Edgar was just, in the belief that 'he associated with the
pro-German party in New York... and identified himself
with them in utterance and in deed'.[14]

'Speyer's affair has made quite a big noise',[15] observed
Carswell, secretary to the Committee, when it produced
its report. Yet this was no Dreyfus case, such as to divide
families, convulse society or put in question the integrity
of the state. No body of opinion emerged to question
Edgar's condemnation. Edgar himself, while protesting
his innocence, announced his acceptance of the outcome
with 'equanimity'.[16] No lessons were drawn from the
affair: it had no repercussions. It was, figuratively and
perhaps literally, a nine days' wonder, a postscript to the
war.

How, then, should it be seen? As a tale of hubris visited on an overweening Titan – 'this great Sir Edgar
Speyer',[17] as H A Gwynne wrote mockingly at the outbreak of the war, or 'the notorious German, Sir Edgar
Speyer',[18] as William Boosey wrote vindictively at its

conclusion? What mischievous sprite had tempted Edgar, on receiving his baronetcy in 1906, to choose for his coat-of-arms a turkey-cock between two trumpeting elephant-trunks, and the ambitious motto: *Arduus ad solem*?* Did he, like Icarus, invite his fate by flying too near the empyrean heights?

To suggest that Edgar and Leonora were to some degree their own worst enemies or that they brought their fate upon themselves would be an exaggeration. Yet there is a residue of truth in it and there was a touch of *folie à deux* in their reactions and their departure for America. In their distress they lacked the instinct of prudence. Unmerited, unfair and humiliating though their social ostracism was, philosophical reflection would have reminded them that their ordeal was little compared to those who truly suffered in the agony of the war. Edgar was hardly what the *Washington Post* described him as on his arrival in America – a 'war refugee'[19] – in the sense applicable, say, to the hordes of wretched civilians who clogged the roads of Belgium in desperate flight from invasion or the reluctant German deportees torn from their English homes into internment camps or, in the case of their English wives and children, into a strange land. And while the Speyers crossed the Atlantic in the comfortable security of a state cabin on a neutral ship, Britons in their thousands were dying in the mud, blood and misery of France and the Dardanelles.

Every cabin on the *SS Philadelphia* was taken when

---

*'striving upwards towards the sun' – Virgil, *Aeneid*, II, 475 she left Liverpool on 26 May 1915. Why did Edgar not ride out the storm rather than cut and run, fleeing, as it appeared to some, his country of adoption in its time of trouble? Mr Justice Salter conceded that 'no adverse inference should be drawn from his leaving this country'.[20] Yet the reproach of cowardice also formed part of the opprobrium hurled at him. It underlies a mocking caricature by the artist and wit, Sir Philip Burne-Jones. Entitled 'The Unholy Family' or '"The Flight into Egypt" 1915', it depicts Edgar as the donkey, ridden into New York by a sprightly, dominant Leonora and led by their young musical protégé, Percy Grainger. Grainger had decamped for America early in the war. Justly rating himself Australia's first composer of worth, he had, as he admitted, no wish to risk his neck in the trenches.

Yet it was easier to point the finger of reproof or mockery than to say precisely what in the circumstances Edgar should or could have done. The press yelled at him to 'leave the country' or 'retire into seclusion'.[21] Where was he to find seclusion in England? In London the mob was howling at his door. As a suspected spy, he was unwelcome at Overstrand. Anxious, above all, for his wife's feelings and his daughters' safety, where could he find seclusion other than overseas? 'I tried', he explained, 'to get out of this atmosphere of suspicion which I could not stand any longer, so I applied for a passport to go away'.[22]

The question of Edgar's motives in leaving for America persists. Did he propose to take up permanent residence there? So claimed *The Sunday Times*, which reported him, on what evidence is not known, as having announced on his departure that 'he never wished to return to this country'.[23] The reason Edgar gave was his need for respite. On arriving in New York, he told the press: 'The anxieties of life in London have worn me out and I require a long rest'.[24] He denied any intention to remain overseas for the duration.

His original destination was not the United States. He had applied for a passport on the day he wrote the letter to Asquith. His wish was to go to Norway, Sweden or Italy, then neutral, but the Passport Office refused his application. Was it feared that he might flee to Germany from these neighbouring countries? If that was his intention, there would have been nothing to prevent him taking ship from the United States to Scandinavia, and thence to Germany. As it was, 'I was informed I could have a passport for the United States, and so I accepted what I could get. I never had any intention of going there'.[25] His first choices of country lend weight to the likelihood that he contemplated a period of repose in natural surroundings free from war; and while he took with him to America some works of art, not suggestive of a short stay, winter clothes were not in his baggage. 'I had no plans', he said at his trial. 'I simply was in despair.'[26] The great London stage on which he had made his career, to smiles and applause, for a quarter of a century, had collapsed beneath him; and at the age of 52 he was struggling, bruised and dazed amid the wreckage, to recover his balance and his sense of identity.

In America, the Speyers stayed in a succession of hotels and rented accommodation, principally in Boston, with holiday houses in Maine. At the same time,

Edgar kept up his houses in Grosvenor Street and at Overstrand. This suggests that he intended no permanent sojourn in the United States. It is true that a letter which he wrote to Eduard in August 1915 suggests otherwise. It reveals his intention, at least at that time, not to return to England except to wind up Speyer Bros. His 'decision stands', he told Eduard. His career in England was over, and while he did not 'lightly give up a position in which he was active for 28 years', he could do no other, and Leonora felt 'the same way'.[27] This sounds definite enough and is consistent with other evidence of an intention not to return to England and even, as the Committee found, to settle in Germany. It is strange that the Crown did not make more of it.

An MP asked in 1916: 'Is there a single chance of Sir Edgar Speyer ever coming back to this country?'[28] Yet the fact is that in the spring of 1918, when the prospect of German victory was at its height he sought permission to return to England, but was fobbed off by Lord Reading in Washington. At the end of the war he moved from Boston to New York, taking a long lease of 22 Washington Square. Leonora, as he very plausibly explained, was tired of hotels and rented houses. He himself returned to London in 1921 to attend the hearings of the Committee, and again, very briefly, in 1924 in the course of a European holiday.

His London house was not requisitioned because the Government could find no use for it. However, in January 1918 Edgar responded immediately and gladly to a private request that it be turned into a convalescent home for limbless officers. This scheme fell through, but he at once agreed to let it as a club for Canadian and South African officers on leave. Edgar himself paid the running costs.

Leonora, née von Stosch, was passionate, susceptible, impulsive and unpredictable. She was a young divorcee when she married Edgar, at a time when divorce was frowned on in England. 'She had charisma and would dominate any room she entered', her granddaughter recalls, and 'was egocentric, difficult, would be either hot or cold, never consistent'.[29] She was, wrote Benson, 'a highly strung woman',[30] with what is called the artistic temperament. *Hell hath no fury like a woman scorned* may be pitching it a little high, as may be the accusation – though it found credence with Margot Asquith among others – that once war broke out 'she became a blazing, uncompromising pro-German'.[31]

Sir Henry Wood recalled:

> Just before they left this country, I was walking with Lady Speyer in Hyde Park. We watched one of the many units of young men marching and drilling. I remember Lady Speyer turning to me and saying: 'My dear Henry, how can these young, untrained boys hope to conquer our armies of trained soldiers? It is dreadful.'[32]

If Leonora really said this – and what better witness than Henry Wood? – it explains much. The observation, though kindly meant, was in the circumstances extraordinarily imprudent, comparable in tactlessness to the Kaiser's dismissal of Britain's 'contemptible little army'.

Leonora's identification with Germany was the height of folly. Stung by the petty humiliations of which overnight she had become the object, Leonora, as Benson says, 'lost her head a little and spoke bitterly and unwisely about the ingratitude and perfidy of the English, when the only possible course was to be silent'.[33]

If Leonora was at fault in being too outspoken, no such reproach could be levelled at Edgar. For nine months he kept silent in the face of insult and provocation. Much good it did him. When he did protest, his famous letter made matters worse. Sir Ernest Cassel, when challenged to demonstrate his loyalty, penned a dignified letter to *The Times* citing his half-century of service to England and his abhorrence of German policy. Contrasting his letter with Edgar's, *The Times*, commented that it behoved men in Edgar's position to 'dissociate themselves, not from British honours, but from German malpractice'.[34] It was true that Cassel could claim, as Edgar could not, that all his male relatives were engaged on Britain's side. Ostracised and deeply hurt, Edgar remained proud and defiant. Not for him propitiatory protestations of loyalty. Yet he clearly felt impelled to make some public statement. At a time of long pent-up emotion, the action was no doubt cathartic. His letter to Asquith was in its way a *cri de coeur*.

All the same, it was read and remembered as truculent and peevish. Sir John Pedder described it to Asquith as 'a bad-tempered letter'.[35] Austin Harrison, anti-German editor of the *English Review*, described it as 'one of the greatest snubs ever offered to a Prime Minister',[36] while *John Bull* denounced it as 'the mailed fist shaken in the face of the British people'.[37] Three years after the event, Lord Lincolnshire, who had been Lord Privy Seal under Asquith, spoke in the House of Lords of 'the brutal and insolent German manner'[38] in which Edgar had treated his high honour.

Edgar had already decided to leave England when he published the offending letter. Before leaving, he presented Henry Wood with the title deeds to the Queen's Hall Orchestra. This sounds like a parting gift. His letter to the Prime Minister, predating his departure by only nine days, was surely intended as a parting shot and indeed a Parthian shot, not indeed at Asquith, who had befriended him, but at the enemies who had rounded on him with such malice, and still more, perhaps, the fair-weather friends who had abandoned him. All the same, it leaves a disagreeable taste, after Asquith had staunchly defended him with his own letter to *The Times*, that Edgar requited him by leaving the country four days later.

Nor was it tactful of Edgar, a fortnight after reaching America, to invite his children's German governess, Fräulein Klock, who had returned home to Kiel on the outbreak of war, to rejoin them in America. Even if it was, in normal circumstances, 'perfectly natural', as he told the Committee, 'that I was anxious to continue the education of my children',[39] circumstances in 1915 were not normal. The Crown did not fail to press home the objection to which Edgar persisted in exposing himself. 'Was it not an extraordinary thing', asked Giveen, 'for a loyal Englishman going to America to import a German governess at that time of the war?' 'No, I do not think so at all',[40] replied Edgar, and denied it repeatedly. Mr Justice Salter was curious. How had Edgar managed to contact Fräulein Klock from America? he asked.

'I sent quite openly a wireless to Miss Klock', replied Edgar.

Mr Justice Salter was incredulous. 'You wirelessed straight to Kiel?'

'Yes, and signed "Edgar Speyer".'[41]

The Speyers did not keep their heads when others around were losing theirs. A sense of proportion, a measure of pluck, a determination to see it through, was missing. Haldane, though he continued to be hissed at in the streets and received more than 2½ thousand abusive letters in a single day, endured his fall in stoical silence. He lived to fight another day, and returned to the woolsack in 1924.

The student of this episode, the reader who has followed the thread of these events, confronts throughout the same fundamental question: was Edgar or was he not a loyal British subject? Asked by his Counsel to explain his attitude in August 1914, Edgar replied: 'My attitude was this: that as soon as Belgium was invaded Great Britain was justified, in fact was obliged to declare war.'[42]

When he resigned as Chairman of the UERL, his successor, Lord George Hamilton, wrote sympathetically that as an Anglo-German Edgar was 'in an absolutely impossible position in the event of war'. 'You have', he concluded, 'been the victim'.[43]

Why, ultimately, had he left England? 'I felt that my usefulness in this country had gone', he said. 'I had not a chance to do anything … I felt that I was only an embarrassment to my friends who stood by me'. As for his war-time sympathies, he replied unhesitatingly:

> My own feelings were, of course, that I stood by my country, England, where I had lived for upwards of 27 years, where all my attachments were, where I spent a very happy time and had great kindness shown me.

Counsel then asked:

> Did the treatment which you received, these accusations of being a spy and a traitor, in any way alter those wishes and attachments that England should win the war?

Edgar replied:

> Certainly not, although of course it made me very bitter. But it did not alter my fundamental feelings of my attachment to England.[44]

How far these sentiments were genuine is for the reader to judge, weighing them against the evidence of this second-hand narrative. Clearly they did not impress Mr Justice Salter, who observed Edgar in the flesh and heard his testimony. It is true that Edgar did not wear his heart on his sleeve or bellow his patriotism from the rooftops, or, as Sir John Simon put it, go around singing 'God Save the King'.[45]

Another target of the protracted campaign against

Edgar was Asquith and the Asquithians. The Prime Minister's Downing Street dinner party in the autumn of 1914, at which the position of the fleet was said to have been discussed in the Speyers' presence, had attained the notoriety of Belshazzar's feast, and in some Conservative eyes, for Asquith the writing was on the wall. 'Was he drunk?' the Earl of Crawford seethed. 'Is he mad, or does he care so little for our Empire?'[46] Crawford's expostulation echoed expressions of mounting discontent at the character of Asquith's wartime leadership. In April 1915 Northcliffe confided 'in violent and contemptuous terms' his misgivings about Asquith, whom he castigated as 'indolent, weak and apathetic'. 'He will never', said Northcliffe, 'finish the war'.[47]

Edgar's departure from these shores and the fall of the last purely Liberal government were coincidental but symbolic of the decline of liberalism generally. The following year, with continuing military failure and deepening public frustration, *John Bull* pilloried Asquith as 'Mr Feeble Hand', and raged against his refusal to legislate 'so that never again shall the Hun-born be able to worm his way into the inner councils of the empire… We want no more Sir Edgar Speyers exalted to the highest rank the State can bestow'.[48]

As late as the summer of 1918, H A Gwynne was still fulminating over 'Mrs Asquith's connection with Speyer',[49] and the charge was revived at the General Election, when Lloyd George and the Conservatives joined forces to defeat Asquith and the Liberals and, as Margot noted:

Herbert Henry Asquith, 'I have known you long, and well enough to estimate at their true value these baseless and malignant imputations'. Asquith to Sir Edgar Speyer, 22 May 1915.

Northcliffe and all who are anti-Henry or me and the
Liberal Party said we were pro-German and Pacifists
from the first day of the war. I would not drop my old
friends for a thousand political ex-enemies. Receiving
Cassel and Speyer (specially the latter...) was fatal to
me among the silly![50]

Edgar was in his way as much a 'scapegoat for Liberalism'[51] as Haldane. In targeting Edgar, Conservatives
were paying off old scores, taking vicarious revenge for
their deep-seated grievances both against Asquith's pre-
war administration and for his wartime failings. In this
sense, Edgar was right in seeing the Committee's Report
as 'neither more nor less than the culmination of years of
political persecution'.[52] The Report gave satisfaction to
Conservatives in its tacit reflection on Asquith and his
public defence of Edgar in 1915 – 'the white-washing
letter', in the words of the *Pall Mall Gazette*, which castigated 'those who raised this imposter to his successive
dignities'.[53] The *Morning Post* did not fail to remind its
readers of 'Mr Asquith's testimony to character'.[54] The
Daily Mail targeted 'Mr Asquith and Sir Edgar Speyer' in
a single headline, deploring 'the fact that Speyer should
have been allowed to gain admittance to the Privy
Council'.[55]

Asquith's motives behind his conspicuous, almost
excessive support for Edgar have given rise to specula-
tion. 'At first glance', writes Professor Brock, 'his loyalty
to Speyer seems wholly admirable'. It was 'brave to invite
him to 10 Downing Street; but given the cloud of enmity
and suspicion that hung over him, was it prudent to

make Edgar a wartime Prime Minister's guest?'[56] Professor Searle agrees:

> Some will admire his stance as showing a loyalty to his friends in their adversity and will applaud his refusal to give way to mob hysteria. Others may doubt the soundness of Asquith's judgment and see this episode as evidence of a supercilious contempt for public opinion which fatally undermined his wartime premiership.

'Why', asks Professor Searle, 'had Asquith taken such risks with his reputation?' There was, he concludes, 'another possible explanation for Asquith's conduct, namely that he was under a personal or a party obligation to the unpopular financier'.[57] The Earl of Crawford, in his fulminations against Asquith's supposed indiscretion, had concluded: 'No sane man and no patriot would dream of talking on such a matter to a German-born and German-speaking financier, *even if under obligations to him*.' [my emphasis – AL] [58]

Edgar had contributed to Liberal Party funds. He was also generous with his stock market tips. Had he befriended Asquith at a personal level? Leo Maxse, indeed, asked whether Edgar, 'the spoilt darling of Downing Street', had bestowed 'Stock Exchange tips à la Marconi'.[59] It is certainly true that, while not embarrassed for money in the conventional sense, the Asquiths always felt the pinch of an income insufficient to their extravagant style of life. The known evidence adds up to very little. In 1910, while his Grosvenor Street house was undergoing redecoration, Edgar had taken a six-month lease on the Asquiths' mansion in Cavendish Square. Whether he paid rent at more than the market rate is not known. The point is that the Asquiths were rumoured to be in hock to their German friends. An anonymous letter to Margot in May 1915 read: '(1) People think you have sold England to the Germans to pay your debts (2) That is why you daren't intern the big Germans.'[60]

Viewed in this light, Speyer's letter to *The Times* might on one reading be understood not merely as a defiant snap of the fingers in the face of public opinion, but as a calling-in of favours from a Prime Minister beholden to him. If there is substance in this hypothesis – for which, it must be emphasised, there is no shred of evidence – to Asquith's instant letter of support may be added the evidence of a cable sent by Edgar from America in August 1915 direct to Asquith in the following terms:

> It seems that many of my cables to London continue to be arbitrarily held up by censor. I strongly protest against such unwarranted action and resent the implied distrust. Moreover my inability of freely communicating with London works to the detriment of British investors.[61]

Was this the language in which to address a Prime Minister – unless the sender felt confident of his standing with him?

But perhaps the most likely explanation of Asquith's

response to Edgar's letter is to be found in the contrast it formed with his simultaneous treatment of Haldane, whom he dropped from his Cabinet, with regret, no doubt, but without ceremony, hesitation or apology, in order to save his own prime-ministerial skin. The day before he wrote to Edgar, he had a tête-à-tête with Haldane, which left him, Margot noted at the time, 'more shattered… than by anything else'[62] in the political crisis of May 1915. Asquith's public letter of support for Edgar, with its fine disdain for press clamour, may have helped assuage the pangs of conscience and the need to reinforce his own self-respect which he certainly felt in throwing Haldane to the wolves. In standing by Edgar at least, he would not be found wanting in the duties of friendship. In a sense, of course, he had no choice. His hand was forced. Edgar's publication of his own letter compelled Asquith to follow suit.

The Privy Councillorship was Edgar's poisoned chalice. No doubt Edgar rued the day he was ever made a Privy Councillor and no doubt he was utterly sincere when in 1915 he asked Asquith – and again in 1918 Lloyd George – to let that cup pass from him. Membership of 'His Majesty's Most Honourable Privy Council' was – and is – a signal distinction and involves an oath of allegiance to the sovereign; but it was not as if Edgar belonged to the narrow circle of those who were actually required to advise the monarch. In the case of men like Edgar, membership was purely honorary and ceremonial. Of the five others who were sworn of the Privy Council on the same day as he and who included, typically, a retired colonial governor, an admiral and a university vice-chancellor, none would have performed other than titular duties.

Was it a case of much ado about nothing? Not to those members of the establishment, notably Sir Almeric Fitzroy, who had expressed sneering disapproval of Speyer's appointment from the first. Already in 1916 and again in July 1918, Conservative MPs rose at Prime Minister's question time to remind the House that Edgar had requested to be relieved of his membership of the Privy Council and to ask whether his wish could not be granted.

The question resurfaced in October 1918, when Edgar unexpectedly renewed his offer of resignation in a telegram to Lloyd George. As has been seen, it landed in Downing Street like the proverbial hot potato. Lloyd George wanted nothing to do with it and lobbed it to the King's Private Secretary. He in turn sought advice from the Lord Chancellor's Department, which 'advised him in effect that he had better ask His Majesty's Ministers, and particularly the Prime Minister and the Home Secretary'.[63] The Home Office debated 'whether he can or should be allowed to take this step'.[64] Opinion oscillated between accepting Edgar's resignation – 'from the point of view of the satisfaction of the public' it would be 'a good thing'[65] – and continuing to trawl for information that would lead to his condemnation by the Committee of enquiry. It was another three years before the desired result was reached. Edgar's real offence lay in treating the honour so lightly by asking to be relieved of it. He could not be permitted to relinquish it on his own terms. He must be deprived of it by due process, and that process would be activated by the revocation of his citizenship. The shining new statutory machinery devised for the purpose must be set in motion. The formalities must be duly gone through. The grim, protracted game must be played out to the end.

Why was Edgar's trial held behind closed doors? It might be supposed that this was another malicious touch by the authorities. The supposition would be wrong. It was true that hearings *in camera* had been the practice of the Committee hitherto; but no other case had aroused the same public interest as this, and both the Home Office and the Crown favoured open proceedings. The Committee had the discretion to authorise either: it was Edgar who requested privacy.

It was a cardinal error. Not only did it give the Committee the obvious impression that he had something to hide, but it deprived him of the vital oxygen of publicity. The press, including the Liberal press, would have attended in force. An open hearing would have enabled those whom the *Manchester Guardian* referred to as his 'many friends here who will entirely refuse to believe' in his guilt and who 'think that Sir Edgar Speyer has been dealt with severely'[66] to hear the evidence and test for themselves both the strength of the allegations and the fairness of the proceedings. As it was, the only source of information was the Committee's Report, leaving the last word with Mr Justice Salter. The findings were damning 'if', as *The Times* said, 'we are to believe that the Report is justified – and we must do so, as a Judge of the High Court presided at the meetings of the Committee'.[67]

There is tragedy in the fall of a great benefactor of

English musical and artistic life, who had basked in the approval of Edwardian society; but that individual tragedy reflects the wider tragedy of a war in which few in the land were untouched. Among the hardest hit were those most closely involved in Edgar's condemnation. The Attorney-General lost his elder son. The Solicitor-General, Mr Justice Salter and the Home Secretary, Edward Shortt, each lost his only son. Edgar's nephew, Karl Schwabach, son of his sister in Berlin, died of wounds in 1916.

Mention has been made of another of Edgar's nephews, Erwin Beit von Speyer, the elder son of Eduard and Lucie. In 1912, having matriculated from the Goethe Gymnasium in Frankfurt, Erwin spent an undergraduate year at New College, Oxford, like his German father and his American uncle. In August 1914 he was called to the colours as a non-commissioned officer in the Seventh Dragoon Regiment of the German army. After the advance into France, he found himself near Arras. On 24 September, three days after his 21st birthday, he was one of a small detachment of cavalrymen who volunteered for a particularly dangerous reconnaissance. He became separated from his comrades. It was thought that he had been wounded and taken prisoner. In the agony of uncertainty, Eduard cabled James in New York for help in finding him. At the request of the State Department, the American Embassy in Paris organised a search-party. Erwin had been killed in action. His name is one of three young German war-dead commemorated on a tablet in New College Chapel.

CHAPTER VIII

Epilogue

There is a stillness here –
After a terror of all raving sounds –
And birds sit close for comfort upon the boughs
Of broken trees.

Leonora Speyer, 'April on the Battlefields', 1919

Du holde Kunst, in wieviel grauen Stunden,
Wo mich des Lebens wilder Kreis umstrickt,
Hast du mein Herz zu warmer Lieb' entzunden,
Hast mich in eine beßre Welt entrückt!

'Thou gentle art, in melancholy hours when life's unruly course has
bound me in, how often hast thou set my heart alight with
warming love, and borne me upwards to a better world.'

Franz von Schober, 'An die Musik', set to music by Schubert

For several years after 1915, the great house in
Grosvenor Street, the music room that once rang
with harmony and the chatter of high society, stood
empty. As on the day he left, the children's toys lay scattered about the nursery, their abandoned books in the
schoolroom. In Edgar's study, prominent on his desk, lay

a large volume, embossed in gold lettering with the words 'Dinner Parties'.

Edgar returned to America in 1921. He had sold his shares in the UERL. Speyer Bros was dissolved in 1922. In 1923 he rejoined Speyer & Co and Speyer-Ellissen. In 1925 he was granted American citizenship. He remained in the United States, apart from trips to Europe, for the rest of his life. From his house in Washington Square, waited on by an English butler and footman, he continued to enjoy a style of life which retained something of Grosvenor Street. 'The aroma of Edwardianism', noted Claud Cockburn, meeting him in 1929, 'still hung about him like the scent of a good cigar'.[1] Edgar was 59 when he returned to America, too young, as he had told Eduard, to remain inactive, but the ten years of life that were left to him seem to have been years of enforced though cultivated leisure.

He affected indifference to his ordeal, dismissing it, Claud Cockburn observed, 'with an amiable shrug'.[2] To Mathilde Verne he wrote:

> I am entirely indifferent to what they say or don't say about me. My reward lies in what I have done, and in the loyalty of people like you, who have preserved a sense of justice, and of the fitness of things. *The others do not matter.*[3]

Time might soften but it did not eradicate the memory. Leonora would sometimes rail at England's ingratitude towards Edgar's contribution to the amenities of London life, the bounty he had lavished in philanthropy and the enrichment of art and music. Music, travel and the acquisition of objets d'art continued no doubt to bring such consolation as they could. But the well-springs of his creativity seem to have dried up and there was bitterness in his heart. Pity was felt at a broken life, blighted hopes and lost illusions. The thought, wrote Mathilde Verne, 'made and makes me flame in anger against his destroyers'.[4]

How is Edgar Speyer remembered? His record, he predicted in his public response to his treatment, 'can be safely left to speak for itself'.[5] But can it? No commemorative plaque alerts the passer-by in Grosvenor Street to the former occupants of No 46. A Mount Speyer stands in drear and dismal solitude amid the wastes of Antarctica – *our mountain!*', as Leonora called it, acknowledging to Captain Scott the unlikelihood of 'our *ever* seeing it';[6] but the Scott Polar Research Institute at Cambridge houses no monument to Edgar. University College, London and the King Edward VII hospital, chief beneficiaries of the Bawden Trust, record nothing of his guiding hand.

Of the millions of commuters on the Underground, few will have heard of the man who saved it from collapse and presided over its completion. When the Promenaders join in Elgar's 'Land of Hope and Glory' or Parry's 'Jerusalem' on the last night of the Proms, they pay homage to the garlanded bust of Sir Henry Wood, but not to his indispensable patron. They will not know that Parry wrote to express to Edgar his shame at the outcry against him, that Elgar wrote to him of 'the indebtedness of the English people to you' as 'a great uplifting force'[7] in the nation's musical life. No. 'He will be chiefly remembered', said his obituary in the *Manchester Guardian*, 'as the man who more than any other was the object of attack by those who sought during the war years to drive out of the country or to have interned every resident of German parentage'.[8]

In February 1932, Edgar returned to Berlin to undergo a minor operation on his nose. He haemorrhaged. The doctors could not stem the flow and he bled to death. It was almost 40 years to the day since he had acquired British nationality and ten years since he lost it, and a year before Hitler became Chancellor of Germany.

Eduard Beit von Speyer died in 1933, leaving one surviving son, younger brother of the son killed in the war, who emigrated the same year with his wife and two sons to Switzerland, and from there to America in 1941. James Speyer died the same year. Faithful to Germany, he had sought to alleviate her plight under the Peace Treaties and was prominent in financing American loans to the Weimar Republic.

Unlike Edgar, Leonora reinvented herself. When arthritis put an end to her career as a violinist, she turned to poetry, so successfully as to win the Pulitzer prize in 1927. Her granddaughter recalls that in after years: 'she did describe her wonderful life in England' and how 'she suffered ostracism when the tide turned against them'. Of their great ordeal, she adds: 'My grandmother rarely spoke of this part of their lives, and when she did so it was brief and bitter.'[9] Leonora died in 1956.

All three of Edgar's daughters, whom the Home

Office had deprived of their British citizenship, eventually returned to England. Pamela, the eldest, married Count Hugo Moy. A few years after their union he was thrown from his horse in a riding accident and killed. She came to live in Sussex, where she died in 1985. His second daughter, Leonora, known as 'Baba', was married for less than a year. She met the concert pianist, Maria Donska, a pupil of Arthur Schnabel, and set up house with her in Kent. She died in 1987. Speyer's youngest daughter, Vivien, came to England as one of the first members of the US Women's Army Auxiliary Corps. She died in 2001, aged 94.

Number 22, Washington Square, where Edgar lived out his life of gilded exile, belongs to New York University. It houses the Institute for the Advanced Study of Law and Justice. The irony would not have been lost on Edgar.

Notes

Abbreviations

BL Bodleian Library

ES Edgar Speyer

Hansard Hansard's Parliamentary Debates

HO (1) Home Office Papers, The National Archives, HO
144/12976/465479

HO (2) Home Office Papers, The National Archives, HO
144/12978/465479

MP Departmental Committee on Certificates of
Naturalisation (Revocation) in the case of Sir Edgar
Speyer. Minutes of Proceedings in London. Transcript 17
October – 7 November 1921. National Archives, TS 27/82

Report Report made to the Secretary of State for the Home
Department by the Certificate of Naturalisation
(Revocation) Committee in the case of Sir Edgar Speyer.
Parliamentary Papers, cmd 1569, 1922, London, H.M.S.O.

TS Treasury Solicitor Papers, The National Archives

Introduction

1. Edvard Grieg, diary, 13 May 1906, Edvard Grieg, *Diaries,
    Articles, Speeches*, ed and tr F Benestad and W H
    Halverson (Peer Gynt Press, Columbus, Ohio: 2001), p
    128
2. *Morning Post*, 18 February 1932
3. Report, p 16
4. *Nottingham Evening Post*, 14 December 1921
5. *The Irish Times*, 18 February 1932

6. *The Times*, 9 January 1922

7. *The Times*, 26 August 1914

8. E F Benson, *As We Were. A Modern Review*, (Longmans, London: 1932), p 250

9. C C Aronsfeld, 'Jewish enemy aliens in England during the First World War', *Jewish Social Studies*, 18 (4) (October 1956) p 283

10. *Asquith's Letters to Venetia Stanley*, ed Michael and Eleanor Brock (Oxford University Press, Oxford: 1982) p 293

11. G R Searle, *A New England? Peace and War 1886–1918* (Oxford University Press, Oxford: 2005) p 773

12. *The Independent*, 23 June 1997; BBC report 1997 (http://www.bbc.co.uk/politics97/news/06/0626/aitken.shtml)

13. Leanne Langley, 'Points of departure: Orchestral Concerts, Urban Transport and Sir Edgar Speyer in Edwardian London (abstract)' (http://www.bbc.co.uk/proms/2007/abouttheproms/conference/conference_abstract.pdf); Leanne Langley, 'Banker, Baronet, Savior, "Spy": Sir Edgar Speyer and the Queen's Hall Proms, 1902–14'. Paper given at 'The Proms and British Musical Life' Conference, The British Library, 23 April 2007 (http://www.leannelangley.co.uk/documents/BankerBaronetSaviourSpy.pdf) [accessed 2011] p 6

14. *Rodriguez v Speyer* [1919] AC 59; A Lentin, *The Last Political Law Lord: Lord Sumner (1859–1934)*, (Cambridge Scholars Publishing, Newcastle upon Tyne: 2008) pp 63–5

15. A Lentin, 'Elective affinities, divided loyalties and Anglo-German victims of World War One: the case of Sir Edgar Speyer', unpublished paper presented at 23rd international conference of the British International

Historians' Group, University of Strathclyde, 10
September 2011

Chapter I: La Belle Epoque

1. MP, 2 November 1921, p 1111
2. Stephen Halliday, *Underground to Everywhere. London's Underground Railway in the Life of the Capital* (Sutton Publishing, London: 2001) p 77
3. Halliday, *Underground to Everywhere*, p 97
4. *The Times*, 24 June 1907
5. *The Times*, 24 June 1907
6. Desmond F Croome and Alan A Jackson, *Rails Through the Clay. A History of London's Tube Railways* (Capital Transport Publishing, Harrow Weald, Middlesex: 1993) p 100.
7. Croome and Jackson, *Rails Through the Clay*, p 80
8. MP, 3 November 1921, p 1253, 27 October, p 748
9. *The Times*, 17 December 1906; Hugh Douglas, *The Underground Story* (Hale, London: 1963) p 157
10. *Daily Mirror*, 20 November 1912
11. *Daily Mirror*, 20 November 1912
12. MP, 27 October 1921, p 749; C Tufton, note, War Office, 4 October 1918, HO (1)
13. http://www.leannelangley.co.uk/documents/BankerBaronetSaviourSpy.pdf
14. *Saturday Review*, 19 March 1927
15. Henry Wood, *My Life of Music* (Gollancx, London: 1938) p 209
16. Wood, *My Life of Music*, p 209
17. Grieg, diary, 13 May 1906, in Grieg, *Diaries Articles Speeches*, p 128
18. Charles M Mount, *John Singer Sargent. A Biography* (Cresset Press, London: 1969) p 265

19. ES to Sir Edward Elgar, 6 November 1902. Worcester Record Office BA5247/5(01). Copy from Harley Library, Southampton University

20. Wood, *My Life of Music*, pp 208, 354, 217

21. Wood, *My Life of Music*, p 217

22. Wood, *My Life of Music*, p 207

23. *Observer*, 13 August and 1 October 1911

24. Wood, *My Life of Music*, p 209

25. *Musical Times*, September 1913; *Observer*, 26 October 1913

26. Robert Falcon Scott to ES, October 1910. D. Crane, *Scott of the Antarctic. A Life of Courage and Tragedy in the Extreme South*, (HarperCollins, London: 2005), p 504

27. Scott to ES, dated March 16, 1912. *Scott's Last Expedition. In Two Volumes. Being the Journals of Captain Scott*, (ed). L. Huxley, vol 1, 1913, p 600

28. Mathilde Verne, *Chords of Remembrance* (Hutchinson, London: 1936), p 153

29. *Pall Mall Gazette*, 1 December 1904

30. Felicie Clare to Home Secretary, 8 December 1921, HO (2)

31. MP 28 October 1921, p 839

32. Wood, *My Life of Music*, p 313

33. Kenneth Rose, *King George V* (Macmillan, London: 1984) p 128

34. Count von Metternich to German Foreign Office, 20 February 1906, *German Diplomatic Documents 1871–1914*, ed Edgar T S Dugdale, vol 2 (Methuen, London: 1930) p 243; Bethmann-Hollweg to Count von Metternich, 3 February 1911, *German Diplomatic Documents*, vol 3, p 374
Margot Asquith, diary, February 1912, BL, MS Eng d 3211

35. Norman Angel, *The Great Illusion. A Study of the Relation of Military Power to National Advantage* (Heinemann, London: 1913) p ix

36. Sir Edgar Speyer, 'Germany and England as Citizens of the World', *England and Germany by Leaders of Public Opinion in Both Empires*, ed L Stein (Williams & Norgate, London: 1912) p 39

37. Sir Almeric Fitzroy, diary, 2 December 1912, *Memoirs*, vol 2 (Hutchinson, London: 1925) p 499

38. James Speyer, 'International Finance as a Power for Peace', *Saturday Evening Post*, 18 November 1905.

39. Stephen Birmingham, *Our Crowd. The Great Jewish Families of New York* (Harper & Row, New York: 1967), p 344

40. Crawford, diary, 13 November 1914, *The Crawford Papers, The Journals of David Lindsay, twenty-seventh Earl of Crawford and tenth Earl of Balcarres 1871–1940 during the years 1871–1940*, ed J Vincent (Manchester University Press, Manchester: 1984) pp 344–5

41. Fitzroy, diary, 24 November 1909, *Memoirs*, vol 1, p 387

42. Nina Grieg to Hanchen Alme, 15 May 1906, Lionel Carley, *Edvard Grieg in England* (Boydell, Woodbridge: 2006) p 367

43. *Musical Times*, 1 August 1914

44. Winston S Churchill, *The World Crisis 1911–1918*, vol 1 (Odhams, London: nd) p 159

45. Mary Soames, *Clementine Churchill. The Biography of a Marriage* (Doubleday, London: 2003), pp 120–21

46. Edward Marsh, 'Before the Axe Fell', *Sunday Times*, 5 February 1939

Chapter II: The Blast of War

1. William Boosey, *Fifty Years of Music* (Ernest Benn, London: 1931) p 106; *The Times*, 1 October 1918
2. *Saturday Review*, 22 August 1914.
3. Wood, *My Life of Music*, p 375; MP, 31 October 1921, p 961
4. MP, 28 October 1921, p 764
5. Memorandum, 'Mr Speyer & Company', March 1918, HO (1)
6. *Altoona Mirror*, 8 August 1914
7. *The Times*, 26 September 1914
8. *The Times*, 26 September 1914
9. *National Review*, November 1914, p 443
10. Crawford, diary, 13 November 1914, *The Crawford Papers*, p 345
11. ES to James Speyer, 22 October 1914, in MP, 4 November 1921, pp 1368, 1370
12. 'Sidelights on the Great War. The Problem of the Speyer', *National Review*, November 1914, p 443
13. Michael Hicks Beach to Leo Maxse, 4 February 1915, in Panikos Panayi, *The Enemy in Our Midst. Germans in Britain during the First World War* (Berg, Oxford: 1991) p 189
14. Max Aitken to Leo Maxse, 8 December 1914, in Panayi, *The Enemy in Our Midst*, pp 188–9
15. ES to James Speyer, 22 October 1914, in MP, 4 November 1921, p 1369
16. Margot Asquith, diary, 12 December 1914, BL, MS Eng d 3211
17. ES to James Speyer, 22 October 1914, in MP, 4 November 1921, p 1369
18. MP, 27 October 1921, p 739

19. MP, 27 and 28 October, 3 November, 1921, pp 741, 784, 743, 1233

20. H A Gwynne to Lady Bathurst, 13 October 1914, *The Rasp of War. The Letters of H A Gwynne to the Countess Bathurst 1914–18*, ed K Wilson (Sidgwick & Jackson, London: 1988) p 40

21. Gwynne to Lady Bathurst, 13 October 1914, *The Rasp of War*, p 40

22. Crawford, diary, 13 November 1914, *The Crawford Papers*, p 344

23. Hicks Beach to Maxse, 4 February 1915, Panayi, *The Enemy in Our Midst*, p 189

24. *National Review*, December 1914, p 590

25. Paul Cohen-Portheim, *Time Stood Still: My Internment in England 1914–1918* (Kemp Hall Press, Oxford: 1931) pp 29–30

26. Margot Asquith, diary, 1918, BL MS Eng d 3216

27. Stephen E Koss, *Lord Haldane. Scapegoat for Liberalism* (Columbia University Press, New York: 1969) p 66

28. 'A Good Innings'. *The Private Papers of Viscount Lee of Fareham*, ed Alan Clark (John Murray, London: 1974) p 135

29. Crawford, diary, 13 November 1914, *The Crawford Papers*, p 345

30. Verne, *Chords of Remembrance*, p 154

31. Special Branch, report, 13 November 1918, HO (1).

32. Major Egbert Napier to Home Secretary, 26 September 1914, HO (1)

33. Vernon Kell to Home Office, 1 October 1914, HO (1)

34. Home Office to Major Napier, 2 October 1914, HO (1)

35. Treasury Department, 1 October 1914 HO (1)

36. *Financial Mail*, 17 October 1914

37. Margot Asquith, diary, 7 November 1914, BL, MS Eng d 3211

38. *National Review*, November 1914, p 443

39. ES to Lord Reading, 8 November 1914, British Library, Reading Papers MSS EUR F118/82/48–9

40. ES to Lord Reading, 8 November 1914, British Library, Reading Papers MSS EUR F118/82/48–9

41. Viscount Sandhurst, diary, 10 November 1914, *From Day to Day 1914–1915*, (Edward Arnold, London: 1928) p 100

42. *The Times*, 12 November 1914

43. Lord Northcliffe to Andrew Bonar Law, 6 November 1914, in Cameron Hazelhurst, *Politicians at War. July 1914 to May 1915. A Prologue to the triumph of Lloyd George* (Cape, London: 1971) p 145

44. *Debate between George S Viereck, editor of 'The Fatherland', New York, and Cecil Chesterton, editor of 'The New Witness', London, on 'Whether the cause of Germany or that of the Allied Powers is just'. 17 January 1915* (The Fatherland Corporation, New York: 1915) p 19

45. MP, 27 October 1921, pp 744, 745

46. MP, 27 October 1921, p 750

47. ES to Sir Edward Elgar, 24 October 1914, Worcester Record Office 705/445/5247/5/VI. Copy in Harland Library, Southampton University.

48. ES to Lord Reading, 8 November 1914, British Library, Reading Papers MSS EUR F118/82/48–9.

49. Benson, *As We Were*, p 249

50. Wood, *My Life of Music*, p 375

51. William Orpen to W R M Lamb, November 1914, Royal Academy Archive RAA/SEC/12/13/1

52. *National Review*, October 1914, p 582

53. MP, 28 October 1921, p 750

54. MP, 28 October 1921, p 842

Chapter III: Hue and Cry

1. MP, 2 November 1921, p 1122
2. Crawford to Leo Maxse, 7 January 1915, in Koss, *Lord Haldane*, p 165
3. MP, 2 November 1921, p 1224
4. *Frankfurter Zeitung*, 8 May 1915.
5. *The Times*, 12 May 1915.
6. Michael MacDonagh, diary, 11 May 1915, *In London During the Great War. The Diary of a Journalist* (Eyre & Spottiswoode, London: 1935) p 62
7. *Morning Post*, 11 May 1915
8. *Pall Mall Gazette*, 13 May 1915; *Manchester Guardian*, 14 May 1915
9. Margot Asquith, diary, 13 May 1915, BL, MS Eng d 3211
10. *Scotsman*, 14 May 1915
11. *Morning Post*, 13 May 1915
12. Hansard, 13 May 1915, 71 H C Deb 71 5s, 1848
13. Charles Hobhouse, diary, 10 May 1915, *Inside Asquith's Cabinet. From the Diaries of Charles Hobhouse*, ed Edward David (John Murray, London: 1977) p 240
14. *The English Review*, December 1915, p 489
15. *Manchester Guardian*, 12 May 1915
16. *Morning Post*, 14 May 1915
17. *Morning Post*, 15 May 1915
18. MP, 27 October 1921, pp 748, 749
19. MP, 28 October 1921, p 839
20. Margot Asquith, diary, 19 May 1915, BL, MS Eng d 3212
21. *Financial Mail*, 23 May 1915
22. 'Letter from London', *New Zealand Truth*, 31 May 1915
23. *The Times*, 20 May 1915
24. 'Letter from London', *New Zealand Truth*, 31 May 1915

25. ES to George Bernard Shaw, 18 June 1915, in Langley, 'Building an Orchestra, Creating an Audience. Robert Newman and the Queen's Hall Promenade Concerts, 1895–1926', in Jenny Doctor and D Wright, *The Proms. A New History* (Thames & Hudson, London: 2007) p 293

26. Margot Asquith, diary, 19 May 1915, BL, MS Eng d 3212

27. Margot Asquith to Haldane, 18 May 1915, in Trevor Wilson, *The Downfall of the Liberal Party 1914–1935* (Collins, London: 1966) p 49

28. Asquith to Sir E Grey, May 1915, in R V F Heuston, *Lives of the Lord Chancellors 1885–1940* (Oxford University Press, Oxford: 1987) p 223

29. George V to Count Mensdorff, 19 October 1924, in Rose, *King George V*, p 173

30. Gwynne to Lady Bathurst, 19 May 1915, *The Rasp of War*, p 94

31. *Morning Post*, 27 May 1915

32. *Financial Mail*, 20 June 1915

33. *Bulletin* (Sidney, New South Wales), in A. Moreton Mandeville, *The House of Speyer. A Candid Criticism of Speyer Flotations* (London: 1915), p 56

34. *National Review*, June 1915, p 513

Chapter IV: On the Trail

1. *Evening Standard*, 23 June 1915; *The Times*, 24 June 1915

2. Cree & Son to Home Secretary, 1 July 1915, HO (1)

3. Fitzroy, diary, 18 December 1915, *Memoirs*, vol 2, pp 613–14

4. Panikos Panayi, 'The British Empire Union in the First World War', *Immigrants & Minorities*, vol 8, March 1989, nos 1–2, p 115

5. *Musical Times*, October 1914, p 625

6. *Manchester Guardian*, 15 July 1915

7. Trevor Wilson, *The Myriad Faces of War, Britain and the Great War, 1914–1918* (Polity Press, Cambridge: 1986) p 198

8. Fitzroy, diary, 7 August 1918, *Memoirs*, vol 2, pp 614, 680

9. MacDonagh, diary, 1 July 1918, in *London During the Great War*, p 305

10. MacDonagh, diary, 11 July 1918, p. 308

11. *The Times*, 15 July 1918.

12. Margot Asquith, diary, July 1918, BL, MS Eng d 3216

13. Hansard, 26 July 1918, 30 H L Deb 5s 1229

14. Hansard, 11 July 1918, 108 H C Deb 5s, 573

15. Hansard, 26 June 1918, 107 H C Deb 5s, 1031

16. MacDonagh, diary, 24 August 1918, *In London During the Great War*, p 309

17. MacDonagh, diary, 24 August 1918, *In London During the Great War*, pp 309–10

18. in A Lentin, *Guilt at Versailles. Lloyd George and the Pre-History of Appeasement* (Methuen, London, 1985), p 4

19. C P Scott, diary, 7–8 August 1918, *The Political Diaries of C P Scott 1911–1928*, ed Trevor Wilson (Collins, London: 1970), p 354

20. MacDonagh, diary, 24 August 1918, *In London During the Great War*, p 311

21. Hansard, 11 July 1918, 108 H C Deb 5s 574

22. Hansard, 18 Nov 1918, H L 32 Deb 168

23. Hansard, 31 October 1918. 110 H C Deb 5s 1591

24. *The Times*, 9 January 1922

25. John Pedder to Sir E Drummond, 17 September 1918, HO (1)

26. Home Office to B Thomson, 1 November 1918, HO (1); Metropolitan Police, Special Branch, Special Report re Sir E Speyer, 16 November 1918, HO (1)

27. John Pedder, 29 October 1918, HO (1)
28. 'Note as to the information supplied by and through the F O', HO (1)
29. MP, 31 October 1921, p 933
30. Foreign Office to C de R Barclay, 4 October 1918, HO (1)
31. John Fisher Williams, 'Sir Edgar Speyer', 11 September 1918, HO (1)
32. A W Riley, memorandum, 12 April 1918, HO (1)
33. Fitzroy, diary, 19 December 1915, *Memoirs*, vol 2, p 614
34. Fitzroy, diary, 19 December 1915, *Memoirs*, vol 2, p 614
35. ES to Lord Reading, 8 November 1914, British Library, Reading Papers MSS EUR F118/82/48–9
36. Lord Reading to Foreign Office, 6 April 1918, HO (1)
37. Foreign Office to Lord Reading, 10 April 1918, HO (1)
38. Foreign Office to C de R Barclay, 4 October 1918, HO (1)
39. Reading to Campbell, 18 May 1918, HO (1)
40. Foreign Office to Campbell, 21 May 1918 HO (2)
41. Karl Muck, letter of 21 July 1916, in MP, 4 November 1921, p 1329
42. 'The Speyers', 22 March 1918, HO (1); MP, 20 October 1921, pp 389, 391
43. in Lentin, *Guilt at Versailles*, p 38
44. Stephen E Koss, *Asquith* (Hamish Hamilton, London: 1985) p 240
45. Robert E Bunselmeyer, *The Cost of the War 1914–1919. British Economic War Aims and the Origins of Reparations* (Archon Books, Hamden, Conn: 1975), p 130
46. *The Times*, 6 December 1918

Chapter V: The Trial (i)

1. C de R Barclay to Foreign Office, 2 January 1919, HO (1).
2. Sir A Dennis to Sir W Thwaites, 15 September 1921, TS 27/80; Report, 30 November 1921, HO (2)

3. Williamson, Hill & Co to Treasury Solicitor, 5 November 1919, TS 27/80
4. Treasury Solicitor to Williamson, Hill & Co, 29 November 1919, TS 27/80
5. Charges against ES, 18 February 1920, HO (2)
6. H M Giveen, 'Preliminary Opinion', 20 August 1921, TS 27/80
7. MP, 3 November 1921, p 1244
8. Home Office, 23 August 1921, HO (2); Foreign Office, August 25 – 5 September 1921, HO (2)
9. MP, 18 October 1921, p 29
10. MP, 25 October 1921, p 496
11. MP, 1 November 1921, pp 992–3
12. MP, 1 November 1921, pp 997–1000
13. ES to James Speyer, 22 October 1914, in MP, 4 November 1921, p 1367
14. MP, 1 November 1921, pp 997–1003
15. Report, p 5
16. *The Times*, 9 January 1922
17. *Manchester Guardian*, 10 November 1914
18. John McDermott, 'Trading with the Enemy: British Business and the Law During the First World War', *Canadian Journal of History*, 32, August, 1997, pp 204–5
19. *The Times*, 9 January 1922
20. *Morning Post*, 7 January 1922
21. MP, 17 October 1921, p 17
22. *The Times*, 9 January 1922
23. *The Times*, 9 January 1922
24. MP, 4 November 1921, p 1414
25. Report, p 5
26. MP, 25 October 1921, pp 530, 533
27. MP, 1 November 1921, p 1027
28. MP, 1 November 1921, p 1030

29. Report, pp 5,6
30. *The Times*, 9 January 1922
31. *The Times*, 9 January 1922
32. MP, 25 October 1921, p 648
33. *Morning Post*, 7 January 1922
34. MP, 3 November 1921, p 1301
35. John McDermott, 'Trading with the Enemy: British Business and the Law During the First World War', *Canadian Journal of History*, 32, August, 1997, pp 207–19; Marc Ferro, *The Great War1914–1918* (Routledge, London: 1991) pp 131–2
36. MP, 28 October 1921, p 847
37. ES to Speyer Bros, 25 June 1915, in MP, 28 October 1921, p 862
38. ES to Speyer Bros, 25 June 1915, in MP, 28 October 1921, pp 862–3
39. ES to Harry Brown, 7 July 1915, in MP, 28 October 1921, p 865
40. MP, 1 November 1921, p 1068
41. MP, 28 October 1921, p 862
42. Report, p 11
43. Report, p 11
44. MP, 4 November 1921, p 1385
45. Report, p 11
46. Report, p 6
47. Report, p 7
48. MP, 3 November 1921, p 1319
49. Report, p 7
50. MP, 28 October 1921, pp 831, 833
51. Report, p 16

Chapter VI: The Trial (ii)

1. Report, p 15

2. Report, p 15
3. MP, 31 October 1921, p 954
4. MP, 31 October 1921, pp 932, 955
5. MP, 31 October 1921, p 933
6. MP, 31 October 1921, p 969
7. MP, 31 October 1921, p 955
8. MP, 31 October 1921, pp 955, 956
9. MP, 31 October 1921, pp 956, 957
10. MP, 31 October 1921, p 963
11. MP, 31 October 1921, p 964
12. *Boston Sunday Globe*, 15 July 1917
13. MP, 25 October 1921, p 500
14. *Providence Daily Journal*, 1 November 1917, in S.S. Kagan, 'Trial By Newspaper: The Strange Case of Dr Karl Muck', *New Jersey Journal of Communication*, 1 (1, Spring 1993) p 55
15. MP, 31 October 1921, p 957
16. MP, 25 October 1921, p 415
17. MP, 20 October 1921, p 348
18. *Providence Daily Journal*, 8 November 1917, in MP, 20 October 1921, p 349
19. MP, 20 October 1921, p 348
20. Report, p 13
21. Eduard Beit von Speyer to ES, 6 March 1916, in MP, 17 October 1921, p 47
22. MP, 1 November 1921, p 1097
23. MP, 2 November 1921, p 1111
24. MP, 28 October 1921, p 874
25. Report, p 12
26. Sir Arthur Salter to Edward Shortt, 17 December 1921, HO (2)
27. MP, 28 October 1921, p 810
28. MP, 1 November 1921, p 1087

29. MP, 7 November 1921, p 1456
30. Report, p 12
31. MP, 4 November 1921, p 1411
32. MP, 3 November 1921, pp 1320–1
33. MP, 4 November 1921, p 1411
34. Report, p 16
35. Sir Arthur Salter to Edward Short, 17 December 1921, HO (2)
36. Oscar Dowson, 29 December 1921, HO (2)
37. *Sunday Times*, 18 December 1921
38. *The Times*, 9 January 1922
39. MP, 3 November 1921, pp 1320–1
40. Report, p 16
41. Sir Arthur Salter to Edward Shortt, 17 December 1921, HO (2)
42. MP, 7 November 1921, p 1447
43. MP, 28 October 1921, pp 836–8
44. Report, p 16
45. Sir John Pedder, 30 November 1921, HO (2)
46. Hansard, 17 July 1918, 109 H C Deb 5s 1167
47. Donald Carswell to Home Office, 28 November 1921, HO (2)
48. *The Times*, 11 November 1935
49. Edward Shortt, 1 December 1921, HO (2)
50. *The Times*, 9 January 1922
51. Pedder, 29 November 1921, HO (2)
52. Pedder, 29 November 1921, HO (2)
53. Dowson, 30 November 1921, HO (2)
54. Pedder, 30 November 1921, HO (2)

Chapter VII: Which of us was to Blame?

1. ES to George Bernard Shaw, 18 June 1915, in Langley, 'Building an Orchestra', ed Doctor and Wright, *The Proms. A New History*, p 293
2. Dowson, minute, 12 December 1921, HO (2)
3. *The Times*, 7 January 1922
4. *Pall Mall Gazette*, 7 January 1922
5. *National Review*, January 1922, p 609
6. *Daily Mail*, 7 January 1922
7. *The Times*, 7 January 1922
8. *Daily Express*, 15 December 1921
9. Francis Hirst to C P Scott, 21 May 1915, *The Political Diaries of C P Scott*, p 125
10. MP, 27 October 1921, p 744
11. Fitzroy, diary, 1 December, 1921, *Memoirs*, vol 2, p 768
12. Fitzroy, diary, 1 December 1922, *Memoirs*, vol 2, p 768
13. Fitzroy, diary, 13 December 1922, *Memoirs*, vol 2, p 770
14. Benson, *As We Were*, p 250
15. Donald Carswell to Oscar Dowson, 15 December 1921, HO (2)
16. *The Times*, 9 January 1922
17. Gwynne to Lady Bathurst, 13 October 1914, *The Rasp of War*, p 40
18. *The Times*, 1 October 1918
19. *Washington Post*, 4 June 1915
20. Report, p 4
21. *Morning Post*, 13 May 1915
22. MP, 27 October 1921, p 755
23. *Sunday Times*, 4 January 1920
24. *Washington Post*, 4 June, 1915
25. MP, 27 October 1921, p 755
26. MP, 27 October 1921, p 756
27. ES to Eduard Beit von Speyer, 12 August 1915, HO (2)

28. Hansard, 31 July 1916 84 H C Deb 5s 2063
29. Gabrielle Thorp to the author, 20 May 2011
30. Benson, *As We Were*, p 250
31. C Tufton, War Office, note, 4 October 1918, HO (1); Margot Asquith, diary, 28 December 1918, BL, MS Eng d 3217
32. Wood, *My Life of Music*, 1938, p 378
33. Benson, *As We Were*, p 250
34. *The Times*, 20 May 1915
35. John Pedder, note, 29 July 1916 HO (1)
36. *English Review*, January 1916, p 84
37. *John Bull*, 19 August 1916
38. Hansard, 2 August 1918, 31 H L Deb 5s, 432
39. MP, 2 November 1921, p 1120
40. MP, 2 November 1921, p 1120
41. MP, 2 November 1921, p 1124
42. MP, 1 November 1921, p 921
43. Lord George Hamilton to ES, 19 May 1915, in MP, 31 October 1921, p 923
44. MP, October 28 1921, pp 765–6
45. MP, p 1322
46. Crawford, diary, 13 November 1914, *The Crawford Papers*, p 345
47. Lord Riddell, diary, 20 April 1915, *The Riddell Diaries. A Selection*, ed J M McEwen (Athlone Press, London: 1986) p 108
48. *John Bull*, 19 August 1916
49. Gwynne to Lady Bathurst, 18 June 1918, *The Rasp of War*, p 293
50. Margot Asquith, diary, 28 December 1918, BL, MS, Eng d 3217
51. Koss, *Lord Haldane. Scapegoat for Liberalism*
52. *The Times*, 9 January 1922

53. *Pall Mall Gazette*, 7 January 1922
54. *Morning Post*, 14 December 1921
55. *Daily Mail*, 15 December 1921
56. Michael and Eleanor Brock (eds), *Asquith's Letters to Venetia Stanley* (Oxford University Press, Oxford: 1982) p 293
57. G R Searle, *Corruption in British Politics 1895–1930* (Clarendon Press, Oxford: 1987) p 246
58. Crawford, diary, 13 November 1914, *The Crawford Papers*, p 345
59. *National Review*, May 1915, pp 564, 562
60. Margot Asquith, diary, 13 May 1915, BL, MS Eng d 3212
61. Report on Speyer & Co, New York, 22 March 1918, HO (1)
62. Margot Asquith, diary, 21 May 1915, BL, MS Eng d 3212
63. Claud Schuster to John Fischer Williams, 13 January 1919, HO (1)
64. Home Office, 1 November 1918, HO (1)
65. Home Office, 1 October 1918, HO (1)
66. *Manchester Guardian*, 14 and 16 December 1921
67. *The Times*, 7 January 1922

Chapter VIII: Epilogue

1. Claud Cockburn, *In Time of Trouble. An Autobiography* (Rupert Hart-Davis, London: 1956), p 177
2. Cockburn, *In Time of Trouble*.
3. ES to Mathilde Verne, c1926, in *Chords of Remembrance*, p 154
4. Verne, *Chords of Remembrance*, p 154
5. *The Times*, 9 January 1922
6. Leonora Speyer to Robert Falcon Scott, 30 September 1906, Scott Polar Research Institute, Cambridge MS 1453/178

7.   Sir Edward Elgar to ES, 23 October 1921, in MP, 28 October 1921, pp 834, 835

8.   *Manchester Guardian*, 18 February 1932

9.   Gabrielle Thorp to the author, 6 February and 19 May 2012

Further Reading

Primary sources*

This book relies heavily on unpublished documents on the Speyer case located in the Home Office and Treasury Solicitor's files in the National Archives at Kew.[†] The report of Mr Justice Salter's Committee of Enquiry (submitted to the Home Secretary on 28 November 1921) was published as a 14-page Parliamentary White Paper: *Report made to the Secretary of State for the Home Department by the Certificates of Naturalisation (Revocation) Committee in the case of Sir Edgar Speyer*. Parliamentary Papers cmd 1569 (H M S O, London: 1922).

Apart from correspondence in the National Archives, I have cited unpublished letters from four other sources: from Leonora Speyer to Robert Falcon Scott (1906) in the Scott Polar Research Institute, Cambridge, from ES to Edward Elgar (October 1914) in the Worcester Record Office (of which I was supplied a copy from Southampton University Library); from ES to Lord Reading (November 1914) in the British Library and from William Orpen to the Secretary of the Royal Academy (November 1914) in the Royal Academy Archives.

---

*Many of the titles listed under primary sources are valuable secondary sources in their own right.
† Photocopies of many of these documents may be consulted in the Archive of the Middle Temple.

Margot Asquith's diaries in the Bodleian Library, Oxford, provide first-hand evidence of wartime anti-German pressures both on ES and on the Asquiths. Of published letters, I have quoted four: two letters (of 1910 and 1912) from Robert Falcon Scott to ES in, respectively, L Huxley (ed), *Scott's Last Expedition. In Two Volumes. Being the Journals of Captain Scott*, vol 1 (Smith Elder, London: 1912) and David Crane, *Scott of the Antarctic. A Life of Courage and Tragedy in the Extreme South* (Harper Collins, London: 2005), a letter from ES to Bernard Shaw (June 1915) in Leanne Langley, 'Building an Orchestra, Creating an Audience. Robert Newman and the Queen's Hall Promenade Concerts, 1895–1926', in *The Proms. A New History*, (ed) Jenny Doctor and D Wright (Thames and Hudson, London: 2007) and from ES to Mathilde Verne (c.1926) in her *Chords of Remembrance* (Hutchinson, London: 1936).

ES's essay, 'Germany and England as Citizens of the World', in *England and Germany by Leaders of Public Opinion in Both Empires*, ed L Stein (Williams & Norgate, London: 1913) pp 35–39 and James Speyer, 'International Finance as a Power for Peace', *Saturday Evening Post*, 18 November 1905, exemplify the brothers' pre-1914 optimism. These essays may be compared with Norman Angel's pre-war classic, *The Great Illusion. A Study of the Relation of Military Power to National Advantage* (Heinemann, London: 1913) and with 'Europe before the War', chapter 2 of John Maynard Keynes's postwar classic, *The Economic Consequences of the Peace* (The Labour Research Department, London: 1920). T S Dugdale (ed), *German Diplomatic Documents 1871–1914*, vols 2–3 (Methuen, London: 1930) contains references to ES as an unofficial Anglo-German diplomatic go-between in London and Berlin. On James Speyer and Kaiser Wilhelm II's grant of a title to Eduard Beit, see Stephen Birmingham, *Our Crowd. The Great Jewish Families of New York* (Harper & Row, New York: 1967). Claud Cockburn, *In Time of Trouble. An Autobiography* (Rupert Hart-Davis, London: 1956) includes a description of ES in New York in 1929.

Charles M Mount, *John Singer Sargent. A Biography* (Cresset Press, London: 1969), to which Leonora Speyer contributed information, affords glimpses of the Speyers' pre-war London life. Desmond F Croome and Alan A Jackson, *Rails Through the Clay. A History of London's Tube Railways* (Capital Transport Publishing, Harrow Weald, Middlesex: 1993), Stephen Halliday, *Underground to Everywhere. London's Underground Railway in the Life of the Capital* (Sutton Publishing, London: 2001) and Hugh Douglas, *The Underground Story* (Hale, London: 1963) all throw light on ES as chairman of the UERL, the company which founded today's London Underground.

Henry Wood describes life with the Speyers in *My Life of Music* (Gollancz, London: 1938). For Grieg's impressions of that life in 1906 see F Benestad and W H Halverson (eds), Edvard Grieg, *Diaries, Articles, Speeches* (Peer Gynt Press, Columbus, Ohio: 2001) and Lionel Carley, *Edvard Grieg in England* (Boydell, Woodbridge: 2006). William Boosey's *Fifty Years of Music* (Ernest Benn, London: 1931) contains venomous comment on ES.

Winston S Churchill's classic *The World Crisis 1911–1918*, vol 1, (Odhams, London: n d) and Mary Soames,

Clementine Churchill. The Biography of a Marriage (Doubleday, London: 2003) describe the Churchills as neighbours of ES at Overstrand during the last days of peace in 1914, to which add Edward Marsh on ES, 'Before the Axe Fell', *Sunday Times*, 5 February 1939.

Sir Almeric Fitzroy, clerk to the Privy Council, did not conceal his vendetta against ES in his *Memoirs*, vols 1–2 (Hutchinson, London: 1925). For Kipling's suspicions of ES in August 1914 see Michael Brock, '"Outside His Art": Rudyard Kipling in Politics', *Kipling Journal*, No 245 (March 1988) pp 9–32. *Debate between George S Viereck, editor of 'The Fatherland', New York, and Cecil Chesterton, editor of 'The New Witness', London, on 'Whether the cause of Germany or that of the Allied Powers is just'*, 17 January 1915 (The Fatherland Corporation, New York: 1915) reveals a vicious attack on ES by Cecil Chesterton. On the anti-German temper in England 1914–18, six diaries are illuminating: John Vincent (ed), *The Crawford Papers. The Journals of David Lindsay, twenty-seventh Earl of Crawford and tenth Earl of Balcarres 1871–1940 during the years 1871–1940* (Manchester University Press, Manchester: 1984), Viscount Sandhurst, *From Day to Day 1914–1915* (Edward Arnold, London: 1928), J M McEwen (ed), *The Riddell Diaries. A Selection* (Athlone Press, London: 1986), Michael Mac-Donagh, *In London During the Great War. The Diary of a Journalist* (Eyre & Spottiswoode, London: 1935) Keith Wilson (ed), *The Rasp of War. The Letters of H A Gwynne to the Countess Bathurst 1914–18* (Sidgwick & Jackson, London: 1988) and Trevor Wilson (ed), *The Political Diaries of C P Scott 1911–1928* (Collins, London: 1970).

Panikos Panayi, *The Enemy in Our Midst. Germans in Britain during the First World War* (Berg, Oxford: 1991) cites hostile comment on ES and is in general the definitive authority on its subject. Paul Cohen-Portheim gives a first-hand account of life for enemy aliens in England in *Time Stood Still: My Internment in England 1914–1918* (Kemp Hall Press, Oxford: 1931). Cameron Hazelhurst, *Politicians at War. July 1914 to May 1915. A Prologue to the triumph of Lloyd George* (Cape, London: 1971) cites Lord Northcliffe on German suspects in England. On Sir George Makgill's Anti-German Union, see Panikos Panayi, 'The British Empire Union in the First World War', *Immigrants & Minorities*, vol 8, Nos 1–2, March 1989, pp 113–28. Lord Charles Beresford's attack on Prince Louis of Battenberg in 1914 is quoted in Alan Clark (ed), *'A Good Innings'. The Private Papers of Viscount Lee of Fareham* (John Murray, London: 1974). For George V's attitude to Germanophobia see Kenneth Rose, *King George V* (Macmillan, London: 1984). Edward David (ed), *Inside Asquith's Cabinet. From the Diaries of Charles Hobhouse* (John Murray, London: 1977) records Cabinet opinion in May 1915. Contemporary comment on Haldane is reproduced in Trevor Wilson, *The Downfall of the Liberal Party 1914–1935* (Collins, London: 1966) and R V F Heuston, *Lives of the Lord Chancellors 1885–1940* (Oxford University Press, Oxford: 1987). For Lloyd George's exploitation of the anti-German temper in 1918 and during the 'coupon election' campaign, there is useful information in Robert E Bunselmeyer, *The Cost of the War 1914–1919. British Economic War Aims and the Origins of Reparations* (Archon Books, Hamden,

Conn: 1975), Stephen E Koss, *Asquith* (Hamish Hamilton, 1985) and A Lentin, *Guilt at Versailles. Lloyd George and the Pre-History of Appeasement*, (Methuen, London: 1985). For Karl Muck and a sceptical view of his alleged activities in America, see Sheldon S Kagan, 'Trial By Newspaper: The Strange Case of Dr Karl Muck', *New Jersey Journal of Communication*, 1 (Spring 1993) pp 50–62.

Hansard's Parliamentary Debates and contemporary newspaper and periodical reports are invaluable. A Moreton Mandeville, *The House of Speyer. A Candid Criticism of Speyer Flotations* (London: 1915) is a collection of critical articles on Speyer Bros from the *Financial Mail*. Other publications cited in this book are: the *Altoona Mirror, Boston Sunday Globe, Daily Mirror, Daily Telegraph, English Review, Evening Standard, Frankfurter Zeitung, Irish Times, John Bull, Manchester Guardian, Morning Post, Musical Times, National Review, New Zealand Truth, Nottingham Evening Post, Observer, Pall Mall Gazette, Providence Daily Journal, Saturday Review, Scotsman, Sunday Times, The Times* and the *Washington Post*.

Secondary sources

Media accounts in 1997 of expulsion from the Privy Council contain erroneous and misleading references to ES: see 'Queen Accepts Aitken's Resignation', British Broadcasting Corporation. http://www.bbc.co.uk/politics97/news/06/0626/aitken.shtml and the *Independent*, 23 June 1997. 'Speyer, Sir Edgar, baronet (1862–1932)', the entry by Herbert Grimsditch in the *Dictionary of National Biography* (Oxford University Press, London: 1949) pp 828–9, is essentially reproduced by Theodore

Barker in the *Oxford Dictionary of National Biography* (Oxford University Press, Oxford: 2004) pp 932–3. A sympathetic summary of the background to the Speyer case appears in E F Benson's *As We Are. A Modern Review* (Hogarth Press, London: 1932) pp 57, 247–51. A succinct but comprehensive résumé of ES's life may be found in the excellent entry published in Wikipedia at the time of writing (of which the principle author is David Cane): 'Sir Edgar Speyer, 1st Baronet', http://en.wikipedia.org/wiki/Edgar_Speyer. Leanne Langley hints at a revisionist view of ES in 'Points of departure: Orchestral Concerts, Urban Transport and Sir Edgar Speyer in Edwardian London (abstract)' (http://www.bbc.co.uk/proms/2007/abouttheproms/conference/conference_abstract.pdf) and enlarges on it in her stimulating piece, 'Banker, Baronet, Savior, "Spy": Sir Edgar Speyer and the Queen's Hall Proms, 1902–14'. Paper given at 'The Proms and British Musical Life' Conference, The British Library, 23 April 2007. (http://www.leannelangley.co.uk/documents/BankerBaronetSaviour-Spy.pdf [accessed date 2011] (I have borrowed from Dr Langley's irresistible precedent for the title of the present account). There is an entry on Leonora Speyer in the *American Dictionary of National Biography*, vol 20 (Oxford University Press, Oxford: 1999) pp 472–3 and the *Oxford Companion to American Literature*.

A brief history of the house of Speyer is provided by Alexander Dietz in *Frankfurter Handelsgeschichte*, vol 2 (Frankfurt am Main: 1925) section 81. ES's influential cousin, the banker Arthur von Gwinner is described in Frederic W Wile, *Men around the Kaiser: The Makers of*

Modern Germnany (Heinemann, London: 1913). For the German-Jewish context in England, see Gerhard Hirschfeld, Aubrey Newman, Arnold Paucker, Peter Pulzer (eds), *Second chance: Two centuries of German-speaking Jews in the United Kingdom* (J C B Mohr, London: 1991) and C C Aronsfeld, 'Jewish enemy aliens in England during the First World War', *Jewish Social Studies*, 18 (4) (October 1956) pp 275–83. On the pre-war Right in England, see J A Thompson and Arthur Media (eds), *Edwardian Conservatism: Five Studies in Adaptation* (Croom Helm, London: 1988), A J A Morris, *The Scaremongers. The Advocacy of War and Rearmament 1896–1914* (Routledge and Kegan Paul, London: 1986) and John A Hutcheson, *Leopold Maxse and the National Review, 1893–1914: right-wing politics and journalism in the Edwardian era* (Garland Publishing, New York: 1989). On the wartime press, see Stephen Koss, *The Rise and Fall of the Political Press in Britain*, vol 2, *The 20th Century* (Hamish Hamilton, London: 1984) and J Lee Thompson, *Politicians, the Press and Propaganda. Lord Northcliffe and the Great War 1914–1919* (Kent State University Press, Kent, Ohio: 1999).

For James Speyer, Count Bernstorff and the supposed German peace initiative of September 1914, see Reinhard R Doerries, *Imperial Challenge. Ambassador Count Bernstorff and German-American Relations, 1908–1917*, tr Christa D Shannon (University of North Carolina Press, Chapel Hill, North Carolina: 1989). John N. Horne and Alan Kramer demonstrate the reality of German atrocities in Belgium in *German Atrocities, 1914: A History of Denial* (New Haven: Yale University Press,

New Haven: 2001). On the *Lusitania* see Thomas A Bailey and Paul B Ryan, *The Lusitania Disaster. An Episode in Modern Warfare and Diplomacy* (The Free Press, New York: 1975) and on the maltreatment of prisoners, Heather Jones, *Violence against Prisoners of War in the First World War: Britain, France and Germany, 1914–1920* (Cambridge University Press: Cambridge: 2011).

The definitive account of the counter-espionage services is Christopher Andrews, *The Defence of the Realm. The Authorised History of MI5* (Allen Lane, London: 2009). John McDermott is helpful on clandestine British trade with Germany, 'Trading with the Enemy: British Business and the Law During the First World War', *Canadian Journal of History*, 32, (August, 1997) pp 201–220 and see too Marc Ferro, *The Great War 1914–1918* (Routledge, London: 1991) pp 130–2.

Stephen E Koss's concise and reliable *Asquith* (Hamish Hamilton, 1985) may be supplemented by George H Cassar's measured reassessment, *Asquith as War Leader* (Hambledon Press, London: 1994) and Roy Jenkins, *Asquith* (Collins, London: 1988). A critical view of Asquith's relations with ES is taken in Michael and Eleanor Brock (eds), *Asquith's Letters to Venetia Stanley*, (Oxford University Press, Oxford: 1982) and in G R Searle, *Corruption in British Politics 1895–1930* (Clarendon Press, Oxford, 1987) and *A New England? Peace and War 1886–1918* (Oxford University Press, Oxford: 2005). On Haldane, Stephen E Koss, *Lord Haldane. Scapegoat for Liberalism* (Columbia University Press: New York: 1969) is definitive. Daphne Bennett, *Margot. A Life of the Countess of Oxford and Asquith* (Arena, London: 1986) remains the standard biography pending publication of Margot Asquith's diaries.

On Lord Reading, see A Lentin, 'Isaacs, Rufus Daniel, first marquess of Reading (1860–1935)', in the *Oxford Dictionary of National Biography*, vol 29 (Oxford University Press, Oxford: 2004) pp 404–11. Mr Justice Salter is mentioned in Alan Hyman, *The Rise and Fall of Horatio Bottomley, The Biographer of a Swindler* (Cassell, London: 1955). There is a concise account of Sir John Simon in R F V Heuston's *Lives of the Lord Chancellors 1940–1970* (Clarendon Press, Oxford: 1987) which may be supplemented by David Dutton, *Simon. A Political Biography of Sir John Simon* (Aurum Press, London: 1992). The critical entry by Robert Stevens on Sir Gordon Hewart in the *Oxford Dictionary of National Biography* is revealing.

In the context of the death of two nephews of ES in the war, Tim Grady, *The German-Jewish Soldiers of the First World War in History and Memory* (Liverpool University Press, Liverpool: 2011) is relevant, or see his 'German Jews in World War I', *History Today*, vol 61, November 2011.

On German deportees from England and their reactions, in addition to Panikos Panayi, *The Enemy in Our Midst. Germans in Britain during the First World War* (Berg, Oxford: 1991), see Nicoletta F Gullace, 'Friends, Aliens and Enemies, *Journal of Social History* (39) 2 (2005) pp 345–67. Philip Hoare, *Wilde's Last Stand: Scandal, Decadence and Conspiracy During the Great War* (Duckworth Overlook, London and New York, 1997), 2nd ed, 2011 places Pemberton Billing's notorious 'Black Book' in context.

For the wider context of the war, Sir Ernest Llewellyn Woodward, *Great Britain and the War of 1914–1918* (Methuen, London: 1967) and Arthur Marwick, *The Deluge. British Society and the First World War* (Palgrave Macmillan, London: 2006) are authoritative studies. The following can all be recommended: Norman Stone, *World War One: A Short History* (Allen Lane, London: 2007) for an introductory conspectus; and the masterly analysis by James Joll and Gorden Martel, *The Origins of the First World War* (Pearson Education, Harlow: 2007); for a valuable narrative of total war, Hew Strachan, *The First World War* (Simon & Schuster, London: 2003); for detailed accounts, Trevor Wilson, *The Myriad Faces of War. Britain and the Great War, 1914–1918* (Polity Press, Cambridge: 1986) and Martin Gilbert, *First World War* (Weidenfeld and Nicolson, London: 1994). For a series of 42 essays on the war and its significance, George A Panichas, (ed) *Promise of Greatness. The War of 1914–1918* (Cassell, London: 1968). The following anthologies are highly readable: Guy Chapman (ed) *Vain Glory. A miscellany of the Great War 1914–1918 written by those who fought in it on each side and on all fronts* (Cassell, London: 1937), Peter Vansittart, (ed), *Voices from the Great War* (Jonathan Cape, London: 1981) and Dominic Hibberd (ed), *The First World War* (Macmillan, London: 1990).

Picture Sources

The author and publisher wish to express their thanks to the following sources of illustrative material and for permission to reproduce it. They will make proper acknowledgements in future editions in the event that any omissions have occurred.

Bettmann/CORBIS p 125, Bodleian Libraries, University of Oxford, Ampleforth Abbey, Serena Thirkell and Toby Crick p 150, Adelson Galleries, New York p 14, Mary Evans Picture Library p 11.

Index